When Stroke Meets Trust

A Journey of Inspiration

Carole Laurin

Ottawa Canada
Carole Laurin

When Stroke Meets Trust: A Journey of Inspiration
© 2013 Carole Laurin
carolelaurin.com
info@carolelaurin.com

First Canadian edition November 2013

Designed by Crowe Creations
crowecreations.ca
Text set in Times New Roman
Headings set in Clarity Gothic SF

Cover design copyright © 2013 by Crowe Creations
Cover photo © 2006 Rygiel Photography

ISBN: 978-0-9920969-1-5

CreateSpace
ISBN-13: 978-1493697236
ISBN-10: 1493697234

I dedicate this journey to Louis, Christian, Chloé, mémère and pépère Laurin, mémère Emond, my whole family, dear friends, and fellow stroke survivors.

Acknowledgements

I owe the completion of this book to my dear friend Stella. I give you many thanks for always believing in my mission to write my manuscript. You never lost sight of my need to honor my soul's contract and you always sent my way the people and resources to help me with this process. I also appreciate your telling me about the Balboa Press writing contest. This was exactly the kick in the pants I needed to complete my manuscript for publishing. I appreciate our precious friendship and benefit greatly from the journeys we share.

I thank Louis, Christian, and Chloé for standing by my side in my darkest hours and for tolerating my personality changes post stroke. I also thank you for your patience and support in affording me all the time I needed to finish this book. Louis, I appreciate and thank you for the tedious job of helping flesh out all the parts of the book I had difficulty editing. I appreciate how you unconditionally accepted my neglect of each of you in the process. I love you.

I am so very grateful to Sherrill Wark of Crowe Creations, whom I serendipitously discovered on-line. You happily took on my last-minute request to edit my manuscript. Thank you, and most of all, I greatly appreciate the exercise in patience I required of you to wait for my edits, to answer all my questions and to alleviate my insecurities about publishing. The final completion of this book would not have been possible without your skills and years of experience as a writer, designer, and editor in the publishing industry.

Mom and my stepdad, Bev, thank you for your continued support to my family and me. Mom, I am grateful for your commitment to be there every day with me for my in-hospital physical rehab appointments and for coming to visit me every day for several months after I returned home. You lifted my spirits in ways I can't describe. To my brother, Dan, and my sister-in-law, Jacqueline, for your unconditional love and help in learning how to deal with my invisible disabilities. Thank you for all your chiropractic care in hospital and throughout my recovery process. To Ivy, my other sister-in-law, who helped in so many ways with your medical advice, unrelenting support, love, and times of laughter, you inspire in me the belief I can still make a difference by launching countless opportunities for me to speak in the professional development of the medical community. To my sister, Denise, and my brother-in-law, Lance, for your support. Denise, I thank you for your efforts to educate others about my cognitive deficits. To ma tante Paulette for always loving me unconditionally and being there at the right moment. To ma tante Doris, for accompanying me to appointments when I was still in my wheelchair and for kindly sewing all my mending when I couldn't do them anymore. To all the members of my extended family, and Louis's family, who have in your special caring ways expressed love and support. Thank you dearly.

Thank you to Mary Eaton, another dear friend who cared for me beyond the call of duty as a therapist and very close friend. Your skills as a physiotherapist and your dedication to my recovery surpassed any expectations. I would not be physically where I am today without your commitment. Thank you, most of all, for our precious friendship and for all the ways that you show me loving kindness and how to be there for others.

To the Rooses thank you for leading us to Joanna Poles. Thank you, Joanna, for working with our family when I returned home from the hospital, and for your companionship and good-natured sense of humor that always brought me laughter while you cared for me. To Liette for your longstanding friendship and for kindly visiting me every week, for several months post stroke, along with your adorable, little Philip. My family and I appreciate you and your generous help with household chores on those weekly visits. To another close friend, Joanne P. whose continued support through regular phone calls following my hospital discharge, and who still does so now regardless of the miles between us always bring me much joy and comfort. To my church ladies, Amabelle, Judy and Chris, who took me out for supper when I was in the hospital and regularly ever since until I moved away. To Carol Carver and Maria Cipriano I appreciate your continuous, cheerful support and friendships. Carol Carver, thank you for helping me find peace through our meditations while visiting in the hospital and at home afterwards. To my neighbor and friend, Audrey, I am grateful for our weekly spiritual discussions; they helped significantly with the final stages of editing by serving to refine my spiritual thoughts and understanding throughout the book.

Thank you Joanne Klassen, my writing mentor, you gave me valuable advice and confidence to begin writing my manuscript for this book. To Rygiel Photography for taking an excellent photo of me that is perfect for my book cover. To Teresa Evans and Master Nona I thank you both for all your insightful teachings and pearls of wisdom when I needed them most.

To my students who made me a beautiful quilt that tenderly warms my heart every time I see it. To my dear colleagues who showered me with love, visits, food, and support, I miss working with you and cherish those life-giving years spent together.

I would need a whole chapter to write about all the people who were generous with their love, time, service, support, and assistance. Therefore, it is with heartfelt appreciation that I thank everyone else who reached out to my family, and me. Your precious pearls of friendships accompanied me along the long road of recovery and continue to do so today.

I am deeply grateful for having the presence of all the people in my life. I am eternally grateful for all who prayed for my family and me especially in our hours of need. God bless you all!

Foreword

The tragedy of life is not that it ends so soon, but that we wait so long to begin it.—Anonymous

My story is not simply about surviving a paralyzing stroke that redefined my life. It is rather how I chose to view this adversity as an opportunity for a new beginning, introspection and growth. By no means had I interpreted my hemiplegia (total paralysis of one side of the body) as an end to life as I once knew it, but as a challenge to forge forward. This mindset helped me discover old and new inner strengths and capabilities to overcome this and any new life challenge.

At some level, I was prepared to survive hemiplegia and at another level terrified I would fail and lose faith in God. Wanting no more losses, I nurtured a mindset that made it possible for me to redefine all adversities as lessons offering valuable blessings. These blessings are my gems that help me get through tough times.

Who would ever say that being suddenly half-paralyzed is a valuable and enriching learning experience? I never imagined I would, moreover affirm this with conviction. Stroke recovery for me set a stage of opportunities for personal growth and newfound wisdom. I could have let myself feel confined and remained physically half-paralyzed. However, the mindful reactions and coping strategies I used gave me the power to affect, resolutely, my body and life's outcomes. This mindfulness, today, is still important for my harmonious daily living.

Oddly enough, stroke recovery taught me how life just doesn't happen to me. I make life happen for me through my choices of how I think and act. Continued determination, attitude, beliefs, and hard work are all part of a great formula for a happy life. While, at times, I lose sight of the fact that how I react to what happens around me determines the outcomes, I do eventually find myself again and reclaim solid ground.

Since my stay in the physical rehabilitation hospital, several people have compelled me to write my story. Therefore, after the hospital discharge, I began to document my stroke experiences by free-writing in a journal. I still wasn't convinced my story was worthy of publishing. As my understanding of my life purpose began to unfold and long-forgotten childhood passions to write were reawakened, I developed a deep knowing that I must write this book. Later in my journey, it became clear why: It was to inspire hope and faith in others facing life-altering challenges.

More importantly, I somehow knew that I had to follow an intuitive process to write, and the outline would come later. As confused and scattered as my thoughts and ideas were, they proved to be very helpful to this book by reminding me what I felt and how I processed my experiences. When I began to convert this journal into a manuscript, it became clear to me that I had instinctively prepared myself long ago for this journey. Since as far back as I can recall, I had blindly chosen certain paths inspired by my inner voice. I say "blindly" because I didn't know then how the journeys and lessons learned from those choices would become helpful motivators throughout my stroke recovery and still are today. Trusting my inner voice often without knowing an outcome was a long-engrained pattern from my adolescence.

Quickly, it became clear that this personal journal would become the bones of a self-help book or, in the least, testimony for my children. As frightening as it was to accept, it was up to me to regain movement in my left-half body. I knew deeply that this journey was significant—that it was the first step toward fulfilling my life purpose to serve God.

This does not mean I was always in control, confident and fearless. But somehow, I always found my way back to being persistent in facing my fears. I needed desperately to prove to myself that I could find inner strengths and courage. My complex journey of stroke recovery was the catalyst toward accomplishing these goals.

I grew to accept my changed body mechanics with astounding inner peace. In the process, my faith strengthened and my spirituality deepened. I cherish knowing that all these acquired learnings continue to help me with life's challenges, inconveniences and disappointments.

Appearances are not always what they seem. My husband Louis's following email to family, friends and colleagues provides brief details about how I began my discovering of a new way of life in the hospital. His email now reminds me how I acted on the surface for others' benefits, to protect them from what was going on inside me.

----- Original Email Message -----
From: Louis Barre
Sent: Monday, November 08, 2004 2:33 AM
Subject: Carole Update -- Day 40

Carole has spent the last two weekends at home with us, returning to the hospital on Sunday evening. Transitioning back home has meant new firsts and new feelings. While home, Carole spends much of her time resting and much of the remainder of her time finding new ways to do old things, such as climbing steps, bathing, getting dressed, performing one handed hair-do's, holding a book and turning pages, and making breakfast. With one arm and one good leg, the most basic activities can be challenging if not seemingly impossible and always time consuming. (A big accomplishment this week was reducing the time to put on her bra from ten minutes to one minute, without pulling it into pieces in the process.) It has often felt like the object or task is too far, too high, too small, too heavy, or just plain too hard and too much! Thankfully, Carole's occupational therapist has taught her some techniques to make life easier and empower her. For example, at "breakfast class" last week, she learned how to butter bread with one hand. And once she has the special cutting board and knife, meant for one-handed people, she expects to be able to slice vegetables with safety and precision. Despite the many frustrations and to her credit, Carole has persisted with determination to relearn these basic tasks. It would be easier to just give up or let others do it for her but this hasn't been Carole's approach.

Louis

Even though I knew I had the love and support from my family and friends, I still felt alone. They couldn't possibly know what I was experiencing at the deepest level. Frightened, feeling alone, and not knowing how I would survive this, I yearned for something greater than myself. The only comfort was God's presence by my side, much like that of a loving parent when a child is scared and helpless. It was as though I knew by magic that acting on this desperate need would be my saving grace.

Shortly after I learned that I had no choice but to find a new way of living, doors opened for writing and speaking engagements. This began unexpectedly with invitations to speak for the Heart & Stroke Foundation, for the Manitoba Stroke Recovery Association, and in the medical communities on such topics as stroke-recovery challenges and interprofessional collaboration for better patient care. As exciting as this was and as appealing to the deprived actor within me, I was nevertheless neglecting my manuscript. In hindsight, this was necessary. These activities ensured that I did not publish before I could prove to myself that what I learned through stroke recovery would be helpful in subsequent, life challenges.

It took more than seven and a half years to complete the manuscript. Through my stroke, I had acquired cognitive deficits and organic fatigue which complicated making sense of my stroke-journal thoughts and other newfound insights. There were many distractions along the way. Speaking engagements, moving twice, and family responsibilities, including attending over a thousand medical and rehab appointments in the four years after my stroke, consumed my energies while I was feeding my mind, and cultivating my spirituality.

A family event that emerged three and a half years into my physical recovery was a most emotional and time-consuming distraction. This event clearly revealed why my unedited manuscript wasn't ready for publishing. This book needed to translate how lessons learned from surviving hemiplegia and hemiparesis (weakness on one side of the body) are indeed helpful in overcoming *any* adversity. These findings were instrumental in achieving a better quality of life.

Until this new direction in my manuscript came along, I was focused solely on explaining my stoke recovery approaches and coping strategies. I knew my scope of audience had widened when I put into practice what I had learned from stroke recovery in overcoming another family crisis and saw how my family and I came out of it not only with grace but unscathed. I had proven that my approaches were valuable gems of life-coping strategies. Not only had I succeeded, but observers had noted how my family and I had been resilient, strong, and optimistic despite two major life adversities. Finally, I knew my stroke story could inspire in readers confidence and hope to face challenges, and would appeal to anyone dealing with a life-altering challenge.

In this book, I choose not to label my challenging journeys as tragedies or crises because that invokes feelings of helplessness instead of empowerment. In sharing my beliefs, practices, approaches, and insights as to how I overcame my life's biggest challenges, I hope I might inspire in others new courage or new ways of coping with theirs.

CL
2012

When Stroke Meets Trust: A Journey of Inspiration

My Insightful Hindsights

Every calling is great when greatly pursued.
—Oliver Wendell Holmes

Searching for Life's Purpose

Ever since I was a little girl, I knew deep in my heart that I was born for a divine purpose or mission. I thought this would naturally reveal itself and once I was an adult, it would come to fruition. However, as time progressed and life's distractions busied me, whatever my calling was to be, became an increasing mystery.

Giving birth to my daughter Chloé when I was 35 years old initiated an intense compulsion that my soul couldn't ignore. I sensed that life as I knew it was going to either change drastically or end at 42. This idea had anchored itself to my mysterious "divine purpose."

A relentless *knowing* that my time was running out had sparked an internal panic that intensified as each year passed. I slowly lost trust that I would find the wisdom and strength to fulfill my purpose before I was 42. I could no longer ignore these compulsions, I had to take some action.

Both the internal timeline and the desire to discover my life mission preoccupied my world. This preoccupation seemed so ferociously irrational that the rest of my life became uncomfortable. It

1

became clear that I was not experiencing mere feelings or thoughts, but more of an inner knowing. Not understanding how to react to this or in whom I might confide, I tried to deny and ignore it. Eventually, this manifested as anxiety. I even told myself I was being dramatic and began to question whether I was losing my mind.

The Quest to Survive

When the pending forty-second birthday was less than two years away, the call to get my life in order became urgent. As it approached, I saw how I had not yet fulfilled my life purpose. This was amplified by a desperate wanting to avert what I feared most: death. This wasn't going to happen on my watch. I took the bull by the horns by setting goals toward achieving a healthier balance between work and family life. Most of all to make a healthier me.

I directed my energies to improving my physical, emotional, and spiritual health. I knew I had to re-engage with God at a more intimate level. I no longer wanted to be distracted from enjoying my family, meditating, praying, exercising, or relaxing because of my career, post-graduate studies, and other distractions.

I recognized intuitively the need to address three things, my physical, psychological, and spiritual health in hopes of having some influence in whatever was to happen at 42. The first step was to build a stronger physical body. I consulted a naturopath doctor. By then, I had stepped into my forties and had gained weight. Fatigue, digestive problems, frequent migraine headaches, anxiety, and what appeared to be the onset of perimenopause plagued me. Under his guidance, I ate more healthily, followed a digestive cleansing regime, lost weight, and felt much better physically.

It wasn't until I had just turned 42 in December 2003 that there was a sense of urgency to focus on the next step, my psychological health. During that time, I was experiencing deep sadness—possibly depression—for approximately six months. I didn't seek medical help because I knew this was a spiritual call, not a physical call for antidepressants. I also had a deep sense of panic about being 42 years old. Not knowing where to go, I began my search with my dear friend and colleague, Stella, who has a doctorate in counseling.

In the spring of 2004, I shared with her how I struggled with being unsettled about my life. She declared that I did not need more talk therapy and pointed out that I had done enough traditional counseling in my past and suggested I needed to "reprogram" my brain into new thinking patterns. Even though I was not sure what this meant, her words resonated with me. I knew instinctively that I needed to do this and I'd find out how. It had finally become clear why I had so often rejected Louis's intended-as-helpful suggestions to seek therapy about my life-purpose compulsion. I needed a non-traditional approach.

Coincidentally, at that time, Louis and I were consulting a child psychologist about parenting questions and approaches. The psychologist observed that I had anxieties and offered an information-processing therapy called E.M.D.R. (Eye Movement Desensitization and Reprocessing). My understanding is that it's a form of therapy to help one's mind naturally unblock and heal itself. I thought this therapy could possibly be what I needed to achieve the goal of changing negative thinking patterns about family, job and, especially, that life-purpose mystery.

The E.M.D.R. treatment involved my wearing headphones that emitted specific sound wave patterns. The doctor would ask me a question and as I focused on it, I had to think of key people in my life while I listened to the sound waves. This process provoked simulated conversations with these significant people—and with God. The conversation that had the most impact was the one with God when the message of my life purpose became clear: I was to serve God. Afterwards, I shared with the psychologist how I was emphatically not impressed with this message. In fact, it had angered me.

I had spent my entire life serving others' needs, all the while neglecting my own. Nothing about *more* service seemed exciting. The idea of serving angered me. I did not want this to be my life's purpose. Aware of my spiritual beliefs and faith in God, the psychologist suggested that I pray and trust that I would come to understand and accept—with peace—my purpose to serve.

Health is a large word. It embraces not the body only, but the mind and spirit as well;... and not today's pain or pleasure alone, but the whole being and outlook of a man.—James H. West

The doctor and I agreed that I didn't need more counseling but I did need spiritual guidance. Hence, the last step of my survival quest was launched. In the weeks following my sessions with the psychologist, I prayed to receive the desire to honor my sacred contract, the wisdom to understand it, the courage to follow through with it, and most of all the acceptance to serve with grace. The E.M.D.R. treatments provoked a positive shift in my thinking patterns. To my amazement, the answers to my prayers unfolded in the months leading to and after a stroke.

Sometime after the E.M.D.R. treatments, a friend asked me to accompany her to an introductory workshop about the mind and body. There, I met three wonderful women who taught me about GeoTran, a healing modality that works with the soul and our divine energies. I volunteered to be the recipient to demonstrate a healing technique. Afterwards, I felt such peace that I had to attend their workshop. Fortunately, the cost did not dissuade Louis to support my need to be there.

Profound Inner Healing

In late August 2004, I attended two GeoTran weekend workshops and experienced a profound spiritual healing as well as a peaceful acceptance of my soul's purpose to serve. I no longer had anxiety or anger about serving God or others. Although I still did not understand what it meant for me to serve, I had self-trust that someday I would unfold this mystery.

I digested some unfinished business about some family members and colleagues and the dark qualities in me that were so-called eating me up. My soul experienced harmony and peace as I de-stressed and my thinking patterns changed in glorious ways. My soul was at peace for the first time in many years. I was grounded and happy to be alive.

New Directions

Following the GeoTran workshops, it became clearer to me that I needed to engage in a regular exercise plan—neglected for too many years. Eating well on its own was insufficient for maintaining a healthy physical body. My demanding and often-stressful career consumed most of my attention and energy. Therefore, I began the new school year committed to exercising.

I thought I'd had good, healthy routines. I was ready for a long life journey. I was armed for my date with destiny. Mostly, I enjoyed reacquainting myself with God through a conscious effort of daily prayer, positive thinking, and the newfound trust in my higher self's inner voice.

By early September, 2004, I was healthy, alive, and most of all, close to God. Although I knew deep in my soul that the unveiling of my life purpose was imminent, I still had peace. Somehow, this insight erased my concerns about that impending change or death at 42. I was convinced that I had misunderstood my compulsion, that all those deep internal stirrings must have been only to invoke a renewed connection with God.

I believed this so strongly that I confidently shared with Louis this new belief. How relieved I was that I had not died and was to be 43 in December. How I learned to let the voice of my higher self (soul) be dominant in my life, and to stop living under the thumb of my ego (lower self). I was elated with my new lease on life.

Good thing, because I had no idea that I was slated for the fight of my life. My date with destiny announced its presence: On September 29, 2004, I survived several TIAs (transient ischemic attacks) and an undetermined number of strokes that left my body half-paralyzed. My strong will to live, God's grace, the loving support of family and friends, and the help of modern medicine granted me a second chance.

I believed immediately that the paralyzing stroke was a catalyst directing me on my spiritual journey in service to God. It was another chance to "fulfill my soul's mission," as the inspirational author, Caroline Myss calls it. She talks about how our soul creates a plan or a blueprint of our life's purpose or mission before we are born. She calls this plan a sacred contract. [Caroline Myss, "Sacred Contracts," 2002]

My Guiding Beliefs

In the earlier edits for this book, I analyzed my thoughts and feelings and discovered that I had intuitively lived by four beliefs throughout my life. However, it wasn't until my stroke recovery that I began to master the living of them consciously. Since my stroke, these beliefs have kept me focused on my life's purpose of service. They drive my commitment to maintain a healthy state of mind and to act wisely during all life's challenges.

Outlined below are the four guiding beliefs that were key to my recovery process and in living life thereafter. These four are each assigned a chapter as are other viewpoints that explain my discoveries and the "gems" of insight I learned during my recovery process.

1. Faith in God (a higher power) and self-trust.
2. There are valuable life lessons in all adversities.
3. Receptivity of mind and soul to attract positive outcomes.
4. Grieve to achieve acceptance and peace

Preceding these chapters is a chapter detailing my actual stroke and hospital experiences in a journal format. Although self-help books typically don't include a journal account of an experience, I think it needs to be here for several reasons. First, my inner voice wouldn't quiet down until I found the right place to insert it even though I still can't fully explain why. I knew Louis's informative and adeptly written emails about my status and experiences while in hospital belonged somewhere in the book. There were countless times his email recipients said his emails needed to be published because of their moving accounts. More important to this book, his renditions about me relate to many topics I discuss throughout the book. They are so delightful to read that sometimes I didn't include my journal entries for those days and placed Louis's emails in the chapter where I write about the actual trauma. I also want to give readers a clear picture of why my physical recovery was such a challenge. Today, except for someone who has experience working or living with people with similar conditions to mine, those who meet me for the first time say they would never have guessed I was hemiplegic. I also wanted to portray my character in trauma so this would give a clearer perspective and a cohesiveness to the book.

Although the journal chapter is abridged, I want to explain why not all my many cherished visitors are not mentioned. My poor memory could not recall when I received you all and I did not know how to compensate for this in the chapter. For the visitors where I did recount our visits, it is because I could piece these events together like a puzzle with the help of Louis's emails. They helped me to remember when I saw family, friends, and colleagues and to recount these visits as I experienced them.

Louis had noted that I had especially confused the order of some events surrounding the first few days following my strokes. I chose to remain with my recollection of the timeline of events instead of the factual accounts because I do not want to compromise the integrity of my memories and my perspectives. I want to recount my experiences as I saw them because it is they that influenced me, not what time I received a treatment or the correct sequence of events.

Essentially, my recovery was not only a physical journey but also a spiritual, psychological, and emotional one. Most importantly, I view each one of these dimensions as a body in their own right with all working together to shape a person as a whole.

The stroke recovery taught me how each of these bodies is critical to recovering a half-paralyzed, physical body. As uniquely distinct as they are from another, they altogether significantly define a whole being. Long ago, when I used to talk about my body, it usually meant only my physical body. Now, it is a collective of bodies.

This might seem an unusual interpretation, however, the North American aboriginal peoples identify human beings as having these same dimensions of self in their medicine wheel. There are other belief systems based on the idea that we have more than a physical body such as etheric (of or pertaining to the ether) or "energy bodies" that relate to the chakras of the body (entry and exit points of flow energy or chi in the energy body). The notion that we are multi-dimensional is universal and not new.

My coping style now is to face stressful situations with thought patterns that nurture healthy, positive reactions. I work hard to find resolutions and not to focus on the problem itself. This means I completely trust that God, Jesus, and all His divine beings will help me see it through to the end. At times, when I face a new crisis or problem I sometimes get distracted from practicing mindful coping strategies but somehow I receive enough messages to remind me I must find ground in my higher self again and stay true to me. I believe that I will and do receive the strength, courage, discernment and all that is necessary to get me to where I best belong, along with the best outcome for others as well as for me.

I had to distract myself from being hyper-focused on suddenly walking and functionally moving my left arm and hand again. Instead, I focused on gratitude and pragmatic positive thoughts, such as any new accomplishment of the day. In the first years, these were minor but nonetheless incremental indicators of physical progress. This focus of thought, however, did not prevent seeds of doubt to sprout. My full trust in God and the people placed in my life saved me from giving up by echoing to me what I had to do to keep my faith, self-trust, and perseverance.

There are many resources that can help us triumph over a life challenge. One way is to acknowledge events. I call them GEMS (pronounced gems). The acronym GEMS translates as Grand Eventual Miraculous Seeds. These GEMS, such as acts of kindness and support, are incremental events that offer us hope, and more, when we most need it. They can be countless events and actions, and be easily overlooked. Each is a mini-miracle. In their collectivity, they contribute to the achievement of goals and healthy outcomes. GEMS are water stations fueling a marathon runner to reach the finish line. The gifts of GEMS fuel us to be inspired, motivated, and/or to be changed. GEMS are seeds of mini-miracles which, when combined, evolve into influential forces. GEMS are miraculous and grand.

There are only two ways to live your life. One is as though nothing is a miracle. The other is as though everything is a miracle.
—Albert Einstein

When I could not see the GEMS or that light at the end of the tunnel after the stroke, I secretly and desperately desired miraculous, mountain-moving events. Even though I believed it unlikely, I kept the view that my glass was half full because I did not want to believe the stroke could be the end of my life as I knew it.

It was then I saw life's small joys as pearls of little miracles, GEMS, and they brightened my days. Often, these GEMS are unnoticed or unappreciated. Each minor victory in my life became a momentous event: sitting up in bed on my own for the first time, winking with my left eye three and a half years after my stroke, or my daughter's success on a test. I had continued to acknowledge the small, joyous events, as countless as they were, as mini-miracles to help me focus on that distant light. This simple act also fueled a positive attitude, smiles, life-giving thoughts, and laughter. Knowing the positive effect thinking this way had on my life, I could no longer take any mini-miracle for granted.

Sometimes the outcome of a prayer or the hope of a goal was not what I had envisioned but usually, more often than not, it was better than what I could have imagined. I chose, and choose, to recognize and appreciate GEMS as part of an impressive choreography of small, but significant events in my life, that are there to help me. They provide my soul with endurance and stamina that in turn give me the determination and grace I need to rise from adversity, much like the mythological phoenix rises from its ashes. Challenges, adversities, traumas, or crises don't happen *to* us, they are there *for* us, to teach us, to help us grow and evolve into better beings, as well as to achieve our full potentials.

The Stroke Journey Begins

The appearance of a disease is swift as an arrow; its disappearance slow, like a thread.—Chinese Proverb

Just When It Seemed
I Was Having a Great Day...

Wednesday, September 29, 2004

The end of another event-filled teaching workday is near. I panic to clean my desk before I leave to pick up my 6-year-old daughter, Chloé, from daycare and to arrive on time for my chiropractic appointment. Louis just then calls me to let me know he is getting Chloé from daycare. He hopes this will allow me more time to get work done before I go to my chiropractic appointment.

Grateful for this extra time in my classroom, I accomplish a few more tasks before I leave for my chiropractic appointment. It's only three weeks into the new school year, and my brain already feels inflamed with fatigue and fogginess. I usually only experience this brain exhaustion after several months into a demanding school year. I also already feel overwhelmed with the mounting teaching responsibilities, meetings, university course assignments, and the lack of hours in a day.

In my car, I listen to a Wayne Dyer inspirational CD to decompress from work as I drive to my brother Dan's chiropractic office where he practices network spinal analysis. Dan tells me that my body is showing good improvement since my minor car accident of last May. This surprises me but I feel relieved given how I feel today. However, I remember telling Louis recently how I felt healthier physically, emotionally, spiritually, and psychologically. Ignoring how my brain feels heavy, I focus on the positive news and feel re-energized.

With my newfound energy, I impulsively detour to a department grocery store on my way home. There are unusually few shoppers, which entices me to shop leisurely in all the store's departments. As I load up my cart with food, household items, and Christmas gifts, my left foot increasingly feels unusually stiff and my toes annoyingly tingly. I think of how a relaxing massage—scheduled for later this evening—will soothe my tired feet and improve my blood circulation. I anticipate even more how this will be a lovely end to a long day. So I think! Little do I know this great feeling is like the calm before the storm!

I decide to drop off the groceries at home before my massage appointment and to bid Chloé a good night. Once again, my left toes bother me but this time they sting like pins and needles. It is so unbearable that I change my shoes before I leave for the massage appointment.

As always, the massage ends too soon. Suddenly, icy cold blood flows through my veins. The therapist reassures me it is from increased blood circulation that is stimulated by the treatment. Accepting her explanation, I focus on how relaxed I am and appreciate the massage's benefits of dissipated tensions. My thoughts wander off to going home to eat a late, light meal and off to bed.

I decide that tonight, I will do no schoolwork or university assignments!

I quickly get dressed in my red suit to warm my chilled body. I always feel great wearing my red suit, which is why I wore it for picture day at school today. As I head out the door, my teeth chatter and my body shivers. I drive home with the car heater on even though it's unusually warm for a fall September night.

9:05 p.m.

The two-minute drive home is not long enough for the car heater to warm my ice-cold bones. It is bizarre how I am still freezing despite the weather. As I climb up our front door steps, teeth a-chatter, the sight of our lovely ceramic planter catches my eye. Remembering I want to take it to work the next day to decorate our school foyer, I securely grasp this heavy planter and struggle to carry it up the limestone steps into the house and up the staircase to my second floor, en suite bathroom.

Leaning over the tub, I carefully deposit the planter into the tub so I can wash away all bugs. Suddenly, I am stricken with a sharp pain in my right temple. I disregard this because I often get these sharp pains. They usually last one to two seconds and are a red flag of a migraine.

An intense but long, shooting pain strikes me again in my right temple as I turn off the water and straighten my body. Only this time, it is so excruciating that my whole body stiffens with pain. I think how atypical this is and almost fear it is an omen. The pain finally stops; I am relieved and decide I must ask Louis what he thinks of this.

I turn around to walk out of the bathroom but I cannot move my left leg forward, it is in spasms; nor can I control its movements. What is happening to me? I reach for the doorframe with my left hand; I also cannot control its movement. It too, is in spasms and both my leg and arm are behaving as though they have a mind of their own. Frightened by what is happening to my body, I call out for help hoping my 17-year-old son, Christian, or Louis can hear me from downstairs. No one answers. I scream again for help. I try to calm down remembering that Chloé is asleep in her room down the hall. I mustn't wake or startle her. Christian arrives upstairs.

The sight of me stifles his typical teenager response, "Wha-a-at!" Immediately, his expression changes from an annoyed one to one of concern.

I tell him to get Louis. "Quickly."

In the meanwhile, my left leg and arm are completely out of control. Worried that any second I'd lose my balance and take a nasty fall, I lean against the door and slide down to the floor. Holding onto my left leg with my right hand, I try to soothe the severe muscle spasms.

When Louis sees me, he asks me if I have hurt my leg.

I look at him and not knowing why, I say in disbelief, "I think I am having a stroke."

By now, the muscles in my face feel bizarre. I think the right side of my face is affected but actually the lost sensation on the left side of my face is what causes the right side to feel distorted. Louis takes one look at me and instructs Christian to call 9-1-1.

Christian runs off without hesitation.

Again, I am freezing with teeth chattering uncontrollably. I don't feel normal and I am confused. I want to cry but all I can do is scream. In hindsight, I cannot control my voice because my vocal cords feel taut. I am trying to talk but I can only produce grunting screeches and intermittent screams.

Apparently, the emergency dispatcher on the phone has heard me and suggests that Louis needs to tell me to calm down and stop screaming.

I want to talk but only screams come out.

Somehow, I'm now lying on our bedroom floor next to our en suite bathroom waiting for the ambulance to arrive. All I can think of is what they will see. I obsess about Louis changing out of his shorts and into long pants. I don't want the emergency responders to see our embarrassingly ugly bathroom that is in dire need of remodeling. I plead with Louis to move me out of our bedroom, but in hindsight, he sensibly doesn't comply.

9:10 p.m.

Within three minutes of our call, the approaching sirens signal the first responders' arrival. The paramedics ask me to raise my arms and do things with my legs. I have difficulty moving them. They confirm this is possibly a stroke and decide to rush me to the hospital.

In the ambulance, the attendant inserts an intravenous catheter and tells me, "We might need this in case you have seizures."

This must be more serious than I think, so I begin to cry. I fear the unknown possibilities and am unprepared to handle them. Worse yet, I might die! I urgently want to bargain with God but our arrival and the activities in the emergency department consume my attention.

9:25 p.m.

My nose is running. I detest runny noses! I need a tissue. Everyone appears too busy for me to ask for a tissue.

Within minutes, Louis arrives at the emergency triage desk. Everything is happening so fast, I'm confused. There is a lot of com-motion: the emergency room is full of people. Many weeks later, I learn there was a man with a stick in his head sitting in the waiting room. I'm glad I didn't know this because I would have realized that if they were making him wait for me, then I must be in serious danger. This would have compounded my fears.

Louis speaks with the ambulance attendant and hospital staff.

What are they discussing? Why is he not yet coming over to see me? At this point, all I care about is getting a darn tissue for my runny nose. I finally get Louis's attention and he finds me a tissue.

Oh, thank you, God. I have full control again of my left arm and hand; I can grab the tissue and blow my nose as I always do, with two hands. I am so relieved I can use both hands now that I'm no longer scared. I tell myself everything is okay. This is all a silly mistake and I can go home. Little do I know that I've had a TIA, a temporary, typical warning sign of an upcoming stroke. These warning signs, by the way, are not meant to be taken lightly.

Nurses attend to me instantly. Wow! I have never before experienced emergency service as fast as this. The neurologist on call this evening happened to be in the emergency department when the paramedics called earlier, and is, fortunately, there to attend to me. We answer his questions. He, too, suspects I am having a stroke.

He tells me about a drug called tPA (tissue plasminogen activator) that breaks down all the blood clots but there is a five percent chance that my brain can hemorrhage. Oh my God! Dying is a real possibility. I do not want to die! I'm too scared to make a decision and so refuse the injection. Obviously, I do not realize how deadly a stroke can be. I assume, in my case, that the chance of dying is probably higher from the medication than from the stroke itself.

My brother, Dan, and sister-in-law, Jackie, arrive in the emergency room. Jackie leaves but Dan stays with me and encourages me to take the drug. Through Dan's and Louis's persuasions, I give my consent for the drug.

In the hustle of blood tests, CAT scans, x-rays, and an MRI, a nurse appears and proceeds to inject the tPA drug into the IV catheter.

She says confidently, "There you go. I am giving you Drano." My concerned look prompts her to explain. "It's a clot buster. Now, your blood will flow like water." She leaves as quickly as she arrived.

My parents' arrival in the emergency room reinforces to me how my situation must be serious. They seem calm and don't appear shocked by my altered appearance. I know that half of my face is drastically drooping. I put on a brave front and try to hide how scared I am. They decide to go into the waiting room. I am relieved because I am not sure how long I can pretend to be brave.

<u>Still within the First Half Hour in the Emergency Room</u>
Sharp pain in my right temple is back. I look at the neurologist and faintly say before I close my eyes, "I think I am having another one." I do not realize at this point that the muscles on the left side of my face have collapsed. My face feels deformed and distorted again. Everything is a blur after this. I think I go unconscious.

Then my bed is in a dark room, deceased relatives and friends surround me. Shining behind them from a rectangular doorway is a light so intensely bright and comforting that I know it is divine. I cannot see facial features but the light illuminates enough that I recognize silhouettes. I fear that their presence is to accompany me safely out of this physical plane, leaving behind my loved ones and life on earth.

The idea of leaving my children and Louis, and family and friends is frightening. It's not right. My children need me. I can't leave them. I'm not ready! I haven't yet fulfilled my life's purpose. I can't go now! I have so much to accomplish!

Fearfully and vehemently, I bellow to God's welcoming committee, "I am not going!"

My eyes open and I'm back in the well-lit ER room with Louis and Dan. I am relieved that my resistance to pass on has succeeded. Did they hear me yell?

I must look frightened because Dan asks me what is wrong.

I panic. If I acknowledge what has happened, they'll reappear. Perhaps succeed with their heavenly mission. I decide to lie. I answer that I have seen my grandfather, Pépère who has let me know I will be fine. I want to believe this myself so I hold onto the lie.

Once again, I experience the same muscle spasms as I did at home. This is not happening only in my limbs but also on the entire left side of my body. And this time, they are intense, excruciating. Each muscle seems to chime in with its own vice grip causing writhing pain until all are pulsing wildly. There is no relief from the relentless spasms. Labor pains do not compare because, at least, I could count on breaks between contractions. The nerves in the brain, as later explained by a neurologist, were damaged and therefore, were misfiring until they could settle down—an agonizing reaction.

I am so exhausted. I can no longer tolerate this painful distress pounding throughout my body. Even though I do not want to complain, I plead with the doctor to do something. He prescribes an antispasmodic medication. Although heavily medicated, I get some temporary moments of relief throughout the night.

The pain wakes me up every time. Louis and Dan are by my side comforting me. I am so thankful to not have to go through this alone. Their presence helps me cope, feel safe, and protected from dying. I need them. I always wondered what it would feel like to have an older brother to look after me. I assume this is what it would be like. I am also relieved that Dan is here to be of support for Louis as well. It is reassuring to know that Louis is not going through this alone. He tells me the children are okay, that his brother, Travis, is caring for them.

Thursday, September 30, 2004

I wake up in intensive care, the room is so dark I think it is night time, but it is morning. Sitting next to me is my friend, Mary. Even though she is a physiotherapist who no longer works in this hospital, I somehow feel she is the best health care provider to have by my side right now. The comfort of her friendship and presence lulls me into a safe zone where I can fall back to sleep.

My sleep is disturbed by physical discomfort. I wake up and I try to roll over in bed but I can't. I am too groggy to know that I've lost the capacity to do this. Mary is perceptive. She notices and offers help. How much easier it is to reposition my body with her assistance! This adds to my fears and confusion: why do I have so little control of my body. Extreme exhaustion pulls me back into deep sleep. Mary is also intuitive. She senses when my body needs a new position and offers assistance. Not only is her presence comforting, but even more so is her help.

Surprisingly, I have a good sleep despite the interruptions of the nurses asking me hourly what my name is, where I am, and what today's date is. I remember that someone has explained that the questions are to ensure that I'm okay. I want to prove to them, and to myself, that I'm okay, so I comply, I answer.

Again, the nurse asks the same questions. I'm getting annoyed because this is one time too many to answer the same darn questions. Can't the nurse see I'm sleeping and too weak to reply?

She is persistent and repeats herself, "Where are you?"

Therefore, I muster up all the energy I have to say, "I am in bed."

The nurse and Mary laugh and I realize she wants to know if I can identify the hospital.

So, I muster up more energy to answer her and go off to sleep.

Later, Mary offers to give me a sponge bath and wash my hair. I accept this because it will feel good. I admire her confidence and how she recruits all the materials she needs from the nurse. She is gentle and respectful while washing me so I do not feel awkward or embarrassed. As she washes my hair, I cannot help but think of Mary as an angel sent to care for me. This act of loving kindness makes me feel even safer. Silently, I thank God for our friendship and her love.

Friday, October 1, 2004

Morning arrives. Mary is gone and Stella is here with Louis. Suddenly, an eager face appears in the unit with her mother in tow. She is one of my precious grade three students who is now in my grade five class. As soon as my heart fills with deep gratitude for her visit, I panic, because I wonder if this means I'm about to die and this is the beginning of the line of goodbyes. Then I think of how the sight of my oxygen and IV lines, and my crooked face must be frightening for her to see. I'm saddened that I can't even pretend to be the able-bodied teacher she knows so well. I'm half paralyzed and I can't chase after her as she runs away crying. I want to comfort her, to reassure her that I will be OK. I feel helpless. I'm not sure if just the sight of me has scared her or if she misinterpreted my look of disappointment as disapproval of her visiting me, instead of my not wanting her to see me in this condition. I hope someday to tell her how much her visit meant to me and that I will always cherish her caring gesture.

Past the point of exhaustion, I force myself to stay awake long enough to answer Stella's questions about my students' work and lessons. I would never have dreamed I could burden another colleague with my work. Even though this ignites guilt, exhaustion drags me into a state where I can't care about this. I know I must let this responsibility go. Right now, survival is paramount.

The medical staff is not compassionate that all I want to do is sleep. The nurses just don't stop waking me to ask where I am, the day of the week and what my name is. Can't they see I need sleep? After all, I know who I am. I don't have amnesia! Little do I understand that after having a stroke or any head injury, waking the patient up for this purpose helps to rule out further brain damage.

Louis arrives and tells me that Shannon, another friend, will be spending the night at my bedside. Why is he making all these arrangements? His worried expression convinces me that I must need someone here with me, even though I resent someone babysitting me.

I rarely see Shannon, so I am honored and wish this were under better circumstances. Ironically, last week, Shannon and I had planned to start scrapbooking this very night with the goal of seeing each other more regularly. I guess we'll have to wait a few weeks to begin this project.

It is generous of her to take time away from her family to spend the night with me in a critical care unit. What a waste of her time! The nurse's desk is right across from my bed. It's too exhausting and confusing to try to understand any more of this. I sleep.

I want to visit and chat with her. I always enjoy listening to her descriptive and entertaining stories. Knowing how I feel, I am incapable of interacting in either language, English or French. Even though a part of me worries that she will be bored, I am too weak and sleepy to think, much less converse.

In retrospect, I am glad Louis arranged for my hospital sitters. I was incapable of knowing if something went wrong. Worse yet, if I needed immediate assistance, how would I go about getting it?

Saturday, October 2, 2004

I open my eyes to find Liette, another very dear friend, sitting in the chair beside my bed. I can't believe Shannon is already gone. I can only guess it must be morning because I remember Louis telling me Liette would arrive at 6:00 a.m. on Saturday.

She shows me a beautifully handcrafted card with impeccable calligraphy. Shannon has made it for me during the night while sitting by my bedside. How very thoughtful. I can't believe I didn't thank her or even say goodbye.

I wish no one has to see all these needles and tubes attached to me. I want to cry and tell Liette how scared I am, but I worry that the sight of me is already an emotional experience for her. I remember many of her extended family members have had stroke. I must look pitiful. I think to myself, don't be so vain. They're your friends and family. They understand.

I am so stiff that I ache all over. Struggling to move, I manage to relieve the discomfort. Repositioning my body in bed is difficult and this is quite disturbing. I'm not sure if the numerous apparatuses attached to my body are complicating this. Let's not forget my overpowering physical fatigue. My body feels as though it has survived an accident.

I wake up still unable to shift my body to one side. It's as though my body is in a straight jacket. Liette tries to help me move but is unsure how she can assist. I remember how Mary helped, so I suggest to Liette how to turn me on my side and reposition my left arm. I am glad she is here, as always she is cheerful, nurturing and positive, but I am so tired I can't help but fall asleep even though I am still uncomfortable.

Later this morning, a physiotherapist arrives to fit me for a left arm sling because my arm just hangs there. The sling is to protect my shoulder tendons, nerves, and flaccid arm muscles. The nurse needs to hold me in a sitting position while the therapist assesses which muscles I can activate on the left side of my body. Pretty much nothing. They move me to a chair next to my bed. I am nauseous. Liette has to hold a kidney pan under my chin while the physiotherapist measures me for the arm sling. It takes forever.

The next dose of prescribed medication overwhelms my body again with severe nausea and fatigue. I am so uncomfortable, I can't engage with anyone. Why can't I understand what people are saying? I have to lie down. Surely, Liette will understand.

I just want to lay my heavy body down, sleep forever, and be left alone. Somehow, laughter wakes me up. I am confused because I'm still sitting in a chair. I hear the therapist tell the nurse and Liette, politely, that I am too confused and dazed to do therapy. The physiotherapist will come back another day when I am coherent enough to respond to her questions.

I am relieved to be finally back in bed but will those nurses just let me sleep? No. They must have it in for me! Darn, there's a young nurse waking me up again while she's changing my urine catheter bag. Oh, now that's worth disturbing my sleep. Thank God, I don't have to get up to go to the washroom. I honestly do not know how I would do it without this attachment. Thank goodness this deed is done and I can go back to sleep.

Now what? I can't see Liette anywhere, she must be gone. I can't believe this is happening again; a nurse and an assistant are placing me in a strange chair with armrests and a hole in the seat that resembles a toilet seat. The nurse's assistant proceeds to undress me. I am naked in a chair with a blanket loosely wrapped around both the chair and me. I am too sick, weak, and exhausted to resist. The last thing I sense is going for a ride and that I'm not dressed for this occasion.

As she wheels me down the hall, I feel a cool draft on my behind. I suspect that the blanket is not covering me. Patients, visitors, and staff are in the hall. Under normal circumstances, I would be upset about exposing myself, but nausea and dizziness make me want to go back to bed and be left alone, in peace.

She wheels me to a tiled room where there are large items stored and which looks like a shower room. It is fitted with a drain in the floor and a showerhead attached to a hose from a wall. I get it now. She wants to give me a shower. The nurse's assistant runs the water and washes my body. She has difficulty washing underneath my left arm because it is held securely in position against my chest and bent at the elbow in a ninety-degree angle. Thank goodness, this toileted chair is on locked wheels and has armrests to support my limp body. I can't fall over as she washes me.

Louis walks in at this moment. I am embarrassed that he sees me so physically helpless. This makes me think of anyone, especially elderly people, who have lost physical independence and how this must be similar to what they feel. How humiliating and undignified.

Louis and the assistant are talking about me but I cannot focus on what they're saying. I feel degraded. We are finished and I cannot believe that she is not dressing me in clothes before going out in the hallway. I hope this time I'm not flashing my behind for curious eyes while she wheels me down the hall. Good thing I couldn't resist this ride. Refreshed. Good to be back in bed.

It's several hours later and I can finally stay awake. The doctor has permitted me to have food for the first time since I arrived. My ravenous appetite is evidenced by my mother's chuckling comments, "Look at you! Eating so fast. It's as though you have never eaten food before."

I realize my table manners are probably poor, so I try to slow down and chew politely despite my insatiable hunger. Who could imagine that hospital eggs could be so delicious? I thoroughly enjoy my lunch and can't wait for the next meal.

The speech pathologist's visit bears unpleasant news. I have to eat mechanically soft food (ground food) until the muscles in my mouth and throat function properly to avoid choking and aspirating my food. Forget anticipating my next meal. Like a baby, I can't sit up and I eat baby food. What's wrong with this picture? Furthermore, I have to do mouth exercises to strengthen the muscles so that I can manip- ulate the food in my mouth, swallow effectively and safely. And, oh yes, I have to practice muscle exercises for a symmetrical smile. So much is lost and so much to do! I'm scared!

It's now evening and before Louis leaves, he lets me know that his brother, Travis, and my sister Denise's husband, Lance, will be here tonight to be by my side. I don't understand why there needs to be someone here with me again, especially two people. I do not want people to see me this way. I'm upset, but I am too shattered and weak to insist otherwise. I can't cope and I'm tired again. I can no longer resist the seducing somnolence that lures my mind and body into unconscious bliss. I wander off and get lost again in deep, drug-induced sleep.

The scrape of a moving chair awakens me and I see sitting beside me my brother-in-law, Travis. I wish he did not have to see me this way. Later on, Lance arrives. I can't believe he has just ended a work shift on the police force and is spending the night here. He must be exhausted. He once was an ambulance attendant and I figure he has probably seen worse than this, so I choose to not worry about how I look. But the fact that he is here, means this must be serious.

No. I can't think about this anymore, it scares me. I'm content to hide in the oblivion of my unconscious sleep.

At home, Louis processes this ordeal by writing an email as a way to eliminate returning a long list of phone calls and to keep everyone informed of my status. He depicts how difficult it is for him, for me and for our whole family to cope and adjust to my stroke.

----- Original Message -----
From: Louis Barre
Sent: Saturday, October 02, 2004 8:55 PM
Subject: Carole Update – Day 4

For those of you who may not know yet, Carole had a major stroke on Wednesday night. For the rest of you, thank you for all your prayers these past few days. I am glad to let you know that Carole is doing well, all considered. She is now on a regular ward. She is sitting up and eating regular food.

Carole has had no damage to the part of the brain affecting memory or speech. So, her mind is completely fine -- which is most important. She experienced a very tiny amount of damage to a critical area of the brain responsible for "motor skills." She is paralyzed on the left side, including her face/mouth, left arm and hand, and left leg. The good news is that she is already regaining movement in her left leg, which is very promising and has brought her great relief and joy! She cries each time she is able to move her leg another inch. It means she will probably walk again. She has minimal movement in her arm or hand at this time. Her doctors say that her recovery will take months and could take as long as two years. They offer no guarantees regarding how much she will recover;

everyone is different. But she does stand a good chance given that she is young and otherwise healthy. In the past few days, I have heard many stories about people, usually much older, who had a stroke and experienced significant recovery. So, we are hopeful.

The doctors do not know what caused the stroke. In less than 24 hours, she had extensive tests including 2 CT scans, MRIs, EKGs, EEGs, Echocardiograms, many blood tests, etc. They have ruled out the most common causes of stroke but haven't figured out what did cause it. They are continuing to do more testing, which will continue into next week. Her care by doctors and nurses has been outstanding and she/we feel that everything possible is being done.

Carole will not be accepting general visitors just yet as she still needs to rest most of the day. Also, she has already begun physiotherapy and soon will begin a very demanding rehab program. So she will need her rest. She is receiving cards and flowers, as of this evening (now that she is on the regular ward). She is on Ward GA5 at the Health Sciences Centre. You can mail cards to me at home and I'll take them to her.

I am doing my best to stay in contact with people by phone and email. However, as you imagine, the response has been overwhelming; each day I receive 20-30 phone messages and emails. That is why I've taken to sending the group email. If you haven't heard back from me, please know that I appreciate your calls and pass them on to Carole! It means a great deal to Carole, and the family, to know all of you care so much. Christian and Chloe are doing fine. They are very well cared for and loved by grandparents, aunts and uncles. For the time being, they are staying at their grandparents as I am at the hospital most of the day.

Many of you have offered to help us, which is wonderful. It means a great deal to us. Thank you. Over the next few months, Carole will need a lot of personal support and encouragement. She has a very tough stretch ahead of her. And, as a family, we will have many hurdles to cross. So, I expect we will be accepting people's offers as we need them.

Thanks again. I'll do my best to stay in touch.
Louis
PS Please feel free to pass on this email

Sunday, October 3, 2004

Travis and Lance are gone. It must be morning because Mary is sitting by my side once again. I don't recall if we talked or when she left. I am distracted by the hectic morning of frequent medical staff visits and their important reports to give me. First, a ward doctor advises me to drink more water otherwise they'll reinsert the IV. This threat scares me because I don't like being chained to a cumbersome tube inserted in my arm; it's so uncomfortable to sleep. Second, a different ward physiotherapist visits me to try on a new arm sling but it is still too large. She promises to come back tomorrow with it correctly altered. I wish I didn't need it. Besides, my arm never moves. Third, a nurse confirms my vital signs are now stable and informs me that I will move to the general ward. It's four days since my arrival in the emergency room and I'm finally alert enough to comprehend and remember something a medical staff says. I am hopeful about my next phase in hospital care. It feels normal to have something to which I can look forward. I am one step closer to getting out again into the real world.

Pleasant surprise. The nurses move me to the general ward early this morning. It must have been an easy transition because I don't recall how it happened. I get confused and forget events. My heavily medicated mind seems to be in a constant groggy, foggy state. However, as I settle in bed, Mary leaves and another friend, Christine, arrives to keep me company. Christine's partner, Reiner, joins us shortly afterwards and not long after that, my other friend—who is like a big brother—arrives, Jan [Danish name pronounced Yan]. Louis assigns this Sunday morning watch to my three friends so he can attend Mass and arrive as soon as he can.

I am capable of being hospitable for the first time because I am awake enough to enjoy my dear friends' cheerful and pleasant company. For the first time, I am having a basic conversation with visitors. For the first time, I am more like me. After they leave, along with Louis, I have the energy and clarity of mind to make the observation of how fortunate I am to have friends who care for me and are there for Louis. It is good to be thinking again about something other than being here.

Louis is happy to hear that the doctor's morning visit prescribed that I sit up three hours a day so I can be eligible for physiotherapy. Eager as he is, Louis persuades me to make the effort. I still don't feel ready for physiotherapy. Sitting up is not easy. First, I cannot do it on my own. Secondly, this activity makes me even more nauseous and reminds me how incapacitated I am. Louis wants me to succeed so he gets the nurse to give me anti-nausea medication. Why is he pushing this?

After the guests leave, the nurse comes in offering to remove the urine bag if I promise to go to the washroom. I agree. This artificial appendage is uncomfortable. I hope she also offers to remove the IV catheter from my arm but unfortunately, this is not to be.

I try to lift my body to a sitting position so I can walk to the washroom, but I'm baffled by my inability to do so. The nurse teaches Louis how to help me get out of bed and into the wheelchair. She leaves me with him to get to the washroom. He places me on the toilet and as he lets go of me to move the wheelchair out, I panic because—to our surprise—I can't hold my body upright. I'm slowly falling over heading right for the floor.

I yell, "Louis, grab me I am falling!"

He grabs me before I hit the floor and calls for the nurse.

The limpness of my body has shocked us both and Louis exits the bathroom as soon as the nurse arrives. What has become of my body, and what does all this mean? Not only can I not even lift my body upright, I can't even maintain a sitting position.

I worry that Louis is disgusted by this revelation, but I need my attention to be on toileting. I can't seem to think plus do something simultaneously. The nurse has to wipe me because my left leg will not cooperate and if I try to reach with my right hand I lose my balance. She then helps me to stand up and advises me to sit back down again because she discovers I am now menstruating. She calls Louis back into the bathroom to hold me while she gets a hygienic napkin. Unbelievable! Why didn't the stroke damage exclude the part of my brain that controls menstruating? That would have been such a blessing.

The nurse and Louis get me safely back to my bed.

Perplexed, I ask Louis, "Why can't I move the left side of my body? I could still control it in the emergency room."

Surprised, Louis looks at me as though I ought to know the answer. "You had several strokes."

I can't believe my ears. I can't wrap my head around this shocking news. Why don't I recall having the final stroke that left me severely paralyzed? Do I have amnesia?

Overwhelmed, I can't even bring myself to contemplate what this means. At that moment, I welcome the distraction of the doctor's unexpected visit and I secretly desire miraculous news. He is here from the rehabilitation hospital to assess if I qualify for their physical rehabilitation program. He returns promptly to happily report that I am accepted and there will be a bed for me next week.

This is news I was not anticipating. I didn't realize I needed to go to a rehab hospital. I'm not as excited as Louis is by this announcement. For the first time, I begin to understand that I am not leaving the hospital any time soon, that this condition I'm in will not go away in a week or two as I expected. I then desperately want to believe that it is in the rehab hospital where my damaged body will revert to its fully functional state.

How long will it be before I can resume my life as it was? Why do have to be here for so long? I ruminate over these thoughts and questions all day. *How long will it be before I get these answers?*

There is no time to dwell on these thoughts and my ensuing emotions because, now, a cheerful physiotherapist walks into my room to take me to the physiotherapy department. Relieved to be the only patient in this newly renovated and quiet atmosphere, I don't have to struggle with hiding my awkward, uncooperative body.

Sitting up makes me dizzy and nauseous. I vomit. Too unstable to sit upright on my own, I fall over. Humpty Dumpty rolls off to one side. The therapist assesses how much muscle strength and movement I have lost. The tiniest movements asked of me are arduous, draining. I am relieved when she finally announces that we are finished. I welcome her help to place me in my chair.

In a strange way, I'm happy that this type of physical trauma has weakened me emotionally so I can't react—or even care strongly about my physical losses. Even better, the heavy sedation provided by the newly prescribed antispasmodic medication numbs my interests and attention to the point where all I can do is sleep, sleep, sleep. Louis shares the same observations so we decide that I will stop the medication.

Monday, October 4, 2004

Louis has scheduled my friend Berthe to lunch hour duties. As I anticipated, her visit is refreshing and energizes me for my next sitters. Later in the afternoon, it's ma tante Donna and mon oncle Claude, my aunt and uncle, who are my social companions. My aunt massages my hands with a scented body cream she has given me along with delicious chocolate treats. They will help me eat my supper and I thoroughly enjoy their company. It's surprising how a simple task like eating can be so complicated without the use of a hand. I never imagined that mealtime could be such an exhausting activity.

My conscious minutes have been increasing to hours and this is making me even more aware of my losses and my changed body. I no longer recognize it. What I see and feel—or rather, *don't* feel on my left side—is surreal. It's as though I have only half a body even though it appears to be all there. Even worse, I have no control over its contorted, unappealing positions. I have many more questions for Louis about what really happened to me.

I have a lot of time to spare and stare at my body. Darn, I have no choice but to face the truth and accept this as who I now am. Looking back at what was is painful so I decide I must learn how to work with what I have become. I hope this rehab place will help me rebuild my body. The process will no doubt be a lonely one because my body is mine and no one can live in it but me. I'm terrified. How on earth will I accomplish this. Getting off the medications means the haziness is clearing but the reality that is creeping into its place is dark. I struggle not to slip into denial and depression. I put on a good front for everyone but inside I am a breath away from desperation.

----- Original Message -----
From: Louis Barre
Sent: Monday, October 04, 2004 11:51 AM
Subject: Carole Update – Day 6
Monday, October 4th

Hi everyone,

Just a quick note to say that Carole is doing well. She is generally more comfortable and resting well. Overall, she is regaining strength and able to maneuver herself with her good arm and good leg quite well. We are quickly learning new routines to get her in and out of bed, etc. She officially starts her physiotherapy today, which we are happy about. I am sure she will find it exhausting but she is anxious to get started on her recovery. She is very strong willed and will work hard to get better! Her spirits have been good.

Unfortunately, she acquired a roommate last night. We were enjoying having the room to ourselves... I kind of liked the bed next to her! Now, I am back to "nights in the chair!" There is a pleasant young man (patient), a gentle soul, who sits outside her door and softly sings. He keeps me amused as I pass by.

At this stage, she is still not receiving visitors and probably will not be until she is in the routine of her rehab program and we know when she needs to rest, etc. However, she would be happy to receive cards. I also pass voice messages on to her (though it may take me some time to get back to you). She is always interested to know who called and what they said. If you send emails for her to me, I'll take them to her and she can read them. Your support means a lot to her.

Thanks again for all your support.
Louis
PS. Life is good. It is not quite what we had planned. But it is still good.

Tuesday, October 5, 2004

I am so nauseous that I sleep until my 11:00 a.m. therapy session. For the first time, I stand up and put weight on my left leg. It does not feel it is a part of my body. How did this happen? How can something so familiar become a stranger? It feels foreign to be scared of your own body. All this fear and eating lunch exhaust me even more. I easily go back to sleep, the only place where I find peace and comfort.

Louis schedules Sandra, our good neighbor, to visit me. She showers me with lovely treats she has purchased on their trip to Europe, and from which they incidentally had returned from the night before my stroke. We chuckled at the fact that their bedroom window was near my front door entrance and how their jet lag caused them to miss all the noise of firemen and paramedics traipsing in an out of my house. We always find something to laugh about.

Wednesday, October 6, 2004

This morning bears the news that I will move to the rehab building sometime this afternoon, a week sooner than expected. Why is Louis so excited? He's not the one going there. Why, it seems he can't wait to get my body working and me out of bed. Me, however, I have no motivation because the queasiness, exhaustion, and paralysis make it difficult to process why my body behaves like dead weight. Will I ever again freely move my body with ease and speed? I think perhaps Louis has unrealistic expectations of this rehab place and most of all of me. What if I fail him? What if I fail me?

On my long wheelchair ride to the rehab wing, I think of my overall experience in the general hospital. I think how overworked the staff seems to be and feel fortunate that Louis was there to attend to my personal needs. If I am going to be in hospital for a long time, I'm content that it will not be on the general hospital ward because for the last few days, the new patient next to me screamed constantly from her chronic pain. In some strange way, hearing her sharp screams made feel lucky. I don't have her pain. Oddly, I believe I got the better deal somehow. It's good I'm moving away from her agony because I have enough of my own. I guess her screams made me want to scream about my reality.

I hope my room isn't across from a noisy nurse's station again. On the other hand, a quieter room in the rehab hospital could make my internal, excruciating and lonely pain more prominent. Regardless, I leave this ward in quiet anticipation of a glorious miracle in the rehab hospital.

I'm relieved the unit assistant selects underground tunnels to transport me to my new destination instead of wheeling around among the regular human traffic flow out there in the world. I don't belong there. This long trip makes me nauseous but being able to clutch the kidney pan against my chest just below my chin gives me some sense of control. The only certainty I feel is the comfort of the kidney pan held tightly in my right hand.

A kind-looking, male nurse on duty greets Louis and me and introduces us to my new roommates. They are a young cheerful 24-year-old woman and a pleasant, chatty woman approximately in her early sixties. The bed next to me is empty. There is already a gift of flowers from one of Louis's colleagues waiting for me in the room. He brings this to my attention but unfortunately, I am overwhelmed by my new long-term living arrangement. I cannot even pretend to share in his enthusiasm. I can't believe the sight of a cookie bouquet is not a welcoming distraction as it once would have been, and that sampling it would not even be tolerable.

Louis loves the large windows in my room and soon I see all my plants overtake the empty windowsill. I cannot wait to get into bed. I am so darn exhausted that all I care about is sleeping. The long trip was too much for me and my damaged body.

Therapy begins tomorrow. I want to believe it is here where I will find a cure. I choose to secretly keep this thought to myself because I don't want someone to tell me the truth if it is otherwise. I can't let my thoughts go there. Not yet! I'm not ready!

----- Original Message -----
From: Louis Barre
Sent: Wednesday, October 06, 2004 12:31 AM
Subject: Carole Update — Day 8

Hi everyone,

Today was a long but good day. In short, Carole was transferred to the Rehab hospital where she will spend the next 4-8 weeks. She will have intensive therapy (several hours per day) which she is keen to begin. She is a very disciplined woman and when she applies her full intention to her recovery we know she will realize the fruits of her labor.

Today, Chloe visited Carole after school, just in time to set up Carole's new room. She arranged all the flowers and cards, organized all Carole's personal supplies, and put everything away in their rightful spots! Then, they did homework together and cuddled. Carole said she felt like she was part of Chloe's life again and Chloe left a happy and content little girl! This will be a new routine each day from this point forward.

Carole is still not accepting visitors until we know her daily routines and energy levels.

In friendship and gratitude,
Louis

Thursday, October 7, 2004

This morning, I can't help thinking that this is my first full day in the rehab hospital. The doctor scheduled me for a TEEG (a trans-esophageal echocardiogram) on October 16, but lucky me, there is an opening today and the ward assistant transports me for the procedure. Louis is not with me because he slept in today. As much as I want him here with me, I'm glad he is getting much-needed rest.

Sitting in my wheelchair, alone, I observe the other patients who are well groomed and ambulating freely with able bodies, and wearing normal clothes. Do they know how fortunate they are to be free moving and physically independent? Suddenly, I am embarrassed because I'm the only person in the waiting room wearing a hospital gown. I quickly become aware that my hair is messy and my face is pale, makeup-less. I am disheveled. I stare as each outpatient walks past me to sit in chairs near me. The presence of their ambulatory bodies besieges me.

A flood of intense sadness contaminates my body and mind with consuming thoughts of my losses. I am now drowning in such despair that I can't hold back tears and I cry uncontrollably. I am grateful that a kind receptionist takes notice and quickly wheels me into a room for privacy. Someone takes the time to comfort me by distracting me with conversation and prepares me for the unpleasant medical procedure. The probe down my esophagus taking images of my heart from different angles distracts me long enough from my emotional trauma that I feel better by the time I return to my room.

Once back in my room, I receive good news. The nurse confirms that I have emptied my bladder thoroughly and states, also, that I no longer need an intravenous catheter in my hand. She finally removes it at noon and I am exhilarated by this new level of freedom. No longer do I have to watch how I move or walk to avoid pain or discomfort from this needle inserted in and fastened to my hand.

The events of this first day in rehab have drained me physically and have been emotionally shattering. I fall into a deep sleep regardless of roommates' activities. As I sleep, a kind nurse gently placing a blanket over my body awakens me. Even my daze can't cloud my thoughts enough to stop me from feeling gratitude toward her. How kind of the nurse to check on me and cover my exhausted and chilled body, too broken to do anything about it. Her care and tenderness make me feel that she is a messenger from God reminding me that I am not alone. This act of kindness makes me believe I will always have someone to comfort me. This nurse doesn't know how far reaching her small act of kindness has affected me, but I do and will thank her next time I see her. I can't right now, I'm too drowsy, and am falling back into a deep sleep again…

Friday, October 8, 2004

Today my family physician visits me in the hospital on her day off, with her baby. Her act of kindness is beyond the call of duty and must be another sign from God that he is sending me support so I may hope to believe I am not alone in this with my family. My family doctor was denied access to my records; she then proceeds to find me in the physiotherapy gymnasium where we have a pleasant and brief chat as her baby naps in the stroller. I am quite upset to discover the rehab ward staff denied her access to my records because I had not signed a permission form. I was unaware this form existed. Had I known I would have signed it the first day I entered the ward. I don't understand why they disallowed her to view my records; it was clearly on file she was my family physician. I am so disappointed this kind gesture was rejected and mishandled. I can't help but feel the clerk or nurse on duty lacked compassion and insight. This upsets me every time I think about it. Maybe my doctor could have provided valuable feedback to me or to the hospital. I'll never know.

---- Original Message -----
From: Louis Barre
Sent: Friday, October 08, 2004 1:45 AM
Subject: Carole Update – Day 10
October 7th

Hi everyone,

Carole is moving her leg quite a lot and her strength is really increasing quickly. She can place weight on it when she stands, with support. We have named it "Bulldozer" as she tries to push Chloe off the bed with it each evening. Her arm continues to take its time. While she has near complete sensation in the arm, there is very little apparent movement yet. It mostly just "hangs around." We have named it "Speedy," expecting that it will "grow into its name" as time passes. As much as we would like to see her arm progress as quickly as her leg, we are not in a panic... we know everything will progress in good time and with hard work. Carole also has to do "smile exercises" to help bring her face back into symmetry. So, at least 40 times each day, she smiles into a mirror. It is fascinating that when she naturally laughs, her facial muscles automatically create her natural full smile. It is only when she consciously tries to force a smile that the left side of her mouth cannot quite lift itself fully. Apparently, it is a different part of the brain that governs the muscles associated with a voluntary versus involuntary smile. So, for the time being, she is not very convincing when she laughs at a bad joke. But, good humor is rewarded with a beautiful smile, as it should be!

We continue to receive messages, cards, emails, flowers, offers for meals and help, prayers and kind wishes daily. The support is incredible and helps to sustain us. Thank you. We are still holding back on visitors as Carole's energy is mostly focused on her recovery and spending time with the kids. Over the next couple of weeks, I expect she will have more energy and can have more visitors.

I'll be back in contact with any major new information. But, it will not likely be daily. If I am not in contact before, have a wonderful Thanksgiving weekend. We certainly plan to!

Louis

Sunday, October 10, 2004

Today, I accomplished two new milestones: I independently transferred myself from the wheelchair to the bed, and while trying to sit up in bed I involuntarily moved my leg. This motivates me to stop looking so disheveled, so I ask Louis to bring my perfume, makeup, hair spray, razor blades, and shaving cream. I want to learn how to shave underneath my arms with one hand.

Monday, October 11, 2004

It's Thanksgiving today and I am going to my mom's for dinner. This is my first outing. How exciting! I can't believe how anticipating such a simple outing can bring me such overwhelming joy. Today, I will be like a normal person, spending time with my family at my parents', and eating normal but delicious food.

This excitement quickly disintegrates when the nurse refuses to let me shower for my first day out of the hospital. The prospect of visiting my family unclean devastates me. The nurse thinks she is kind by telling me in a soft voice, which nevertheless seems condescending, to explain I cannot always have what I want... It does not matter how she delivers her chastising lesson about shower schedules, the message is the same, and it is disturbing. Sobbing, I immediately call Louis. He speeds to the hospital to rush me to my mom's for a shower before the rest of the family arrives. My mom is attentive and helpful, and her feminine touch, followed by Louis' gentle help in showering and dressing me, brings me to a state of mind where I feel pretty and human once again, and most of all, presentable. Incidentally, all this rushing caused Louis to get a speeding ticket from a photo radar. Some weeks later, Louis played the stroke card at traffic court but unfortunately the judge wouldn't cancel the ticket.

I am grateful to have a normal day with my children, husband, and extended family. My sister, Denise, offers me a nurturing treat to paint my toenails. She knows how I always kept my nails painted and does this nice gesture to help me feel even better. It's amazing how she is very patient with the spasms in my left toes and foot as the calm nurse in her confidently and securely holds down my left toes to restrain the involuntary spasms for toenail painting.

The best part of the day is eating a real meal with an array of long-missed flavors and textures that delight my taste buds unlike the bland and mushy hospital food. This truly is a day of thanksgiving! I am alive, well fed and well loved. Delighting in the simple pleasures and what I once took for granted is now going to be my new way of living.

Tuesday, October 12, 2004

I reflect on the past days' experiences, such as the nurse–shower incident, and I realize it is from here on out that my healing is in the hands of others who may not understand my losses, needs, and my perspectives. We discover with the resident doctor that I continue to have TIAs because I see flashing lights traveling from the left to the right of my field of vision. Now, I have to take the prescription Plavix, an anticoagulant, because it seems aspirin is insufficient to protect me from future strokes.

In therapy, I am ecstatic: I can take three steps forward and three steps backward. Wow! How bizarre it is to relearn something as automatic as taking a step, something I don't recall learning in the first place, as a toddler. The therapist tells me, I might be able to walk with a cane next week! Wow! This is great possibility! I secretly decide with Louis that it's now time to set my first personal goal, that of walking with a cane by the end of next week. If successful, he will reward me with a hamburger from my old, local famous burger takeout, the Greek's. I know this is not the best thing for cholesterol, but I want a reward for eating the tasteless, ground-up meals I have been getting in the hospital. I choose this to be our secret because I don't want to hear any medical care provider say this is unrealistic and jinx my success. I decide I will share my goal once it appears I have good chance at accomplishing it.

-----Original Message-----
From: Louis Barre
Sent: October 12, 2004 2:49 AM
Subject: Carole update -- Day 14

Hi everyone,

I feel compelled to update you as my "inbox" continues to brim with thanksgiving wishes and interests in Carole's recovery. Thank you.

Carole was able to join the family for thanksgiving dinner at her parents, which was wonderful. It was great for her to get out of the hospital for a few hours, into some real clothes, to eat some real food, and to enjoy a variety of real conversations. It was a bit tough for her to "sit and be served" given her usual helpful and productive nature, but she enjoyed the sunshine and having her toenails painted (there are some advantages). At some level, I am sure, it appealed to the latent princess within her!

As the evening ended, Carole slid out of her nice outfit, took off her beautiful jewelry, and climbed (with my help) back into her prison wear -- green khaki pants stamped in big red letters with "WRHA Laundry June 2004." Then we rolled her back to her room at the hospital. There was a certain level of comfort as she snuggled back into the safety of her hospital bed. She and the lady in the next bed (who also had a pass to leave the hospital) talked about how great the "real turkey" tasted, and how they could in fact chew "real meat" despite what the hospital dietician thinks and that it still gets stuck in their cheeks. (Carole is still officially on a "mechanical soft" diet which sounds better than it tastes. Those of you who know me know that I'll pretty much eat anything that's not nailed down, but I got to say that they serve some pretty nasty stuff! The odd dish is not too bad.) "Bad food" is the subject of a lot of the conversations on the ward... who knows... that's maybe why they serve it... to give the patients something in common to talk about. (The other thing they often talk about is the poor lady down the hall who screams insensibly about 200 times per day. She reminds them just how lucky "they" are, in case they forget!)

In terms of her recovery, Carole has gained a lot of movement and strength in her left leg, which keeps her spirits up. She is already able to place some standing weight on it and is quite easily able to transfer herself in and out of bed. It also enables her to make speedy toilet transfers in the two washrooms that are shared between 30 patients -- which staff and patients roll in and out with no forewarning... you never quite know who is going to see what so you have to move quickly and look straight ahead! We've had some of our best laughs in the bathroom. (This could be the subject of its own email.)

"Speedy," her left arm, is a different story. It does not seem to be in too much of a rush... a late bloomer, we expect. In the meantime, we are just trying to keep it from getting into any trouble... causing a sore shoulder, getting caught between the bed rails, and so forth. Carole feels complete sensation and pain in her arm so it does have some presence and can not be left too far behind without letting her know. Good news, however, she did have a tiny amount of movement in it with her physiotherapist on Friday. So that was encouraging. I am sure she will experience more good progress this week.

Friends and family continue to be wonderfully supportive. Indeed, there is much for us to be thankful for this weekend. We need only look around to see (and feel) how blessed we truly are.

I hope all of you had a great thanksgiving as well.

Louis

PS... times we laughed in the past few days... when I lowered the hospital bed on Carole's bad foot and she was complaining about why she could not climb into bed... and when she flooded the toilet with her first good BM in several days... I said, "Hey babe, you are on your own with this one. I claim no responsibility for the mess we are leaving behind. Let's get out of here before anyone sees us!"

PPS... if you are tired of my musings, please feel free to block me or tell me to take you "off the list." I will not be offended. If not, I will continue to send them periodically, so long as someone is listening...

Wednesday, October 13, 2004

How magnificent! I, today, walked a far and exhausting distance of 10 steps! I could also move my left triceps by lifting my arm outward that still remains locked in a ninety-degree angle at my elbow. Even more exciting, the speech therapist lifts the mechanical diet ban. Now I can look forward to an even more promising hamburger!

Mom announces that she will come to the hospital every day to assist and support me in therapy. She made this decision after a discussion with her cousin whose husband also had a stroke and learned how daily family support will help me face the demanding challenges in physiotherapy and occupational therapy. Happy and relieved to hear this, I am also concerned this will be too demanding for her. I can't worry about this right now because the reality of my physical recovery demands is overpoweringly frightening and daunting. I know I can't do this alone and consider myself extremely fortunate and blessed that Mom will be here with me. I choose to see this as another sign from God.

Thursday, October 14, 2004

Progress is happening! I walked 20 steps forward and backward with my therapist tethered to me with a Velcro belt fastened around my waist. Like a puppy on a leash, I can be steered when necessary, but mainly she can rescue me from falling forward. We are both excited. This means my legs are getting stronger and I can try standing up from a seated position. My father-in-law, Albert, witnesses these struggles. He appears very proud to see me accomplish this, but I sense this is difficult for him to watch because I also see him fight back tears.

Friday, October 15, 2004

My 86-year-old mémère Laurin visits me with my mom and Aunt

Lucille, her sister. They attend therapy with me and cheer me on. I find it bizarre that I show my grandmother how to walk with a cane. What a bizarre and unexpected role reversal! I can't imagine what she must be thinking. It's so good to see them, their smiles, and as always share laughter. I am so energized by their visit.

The bounteousness of family and friends continues to amaze me and makes me feel even more blessed. This evening, close, fun friends of ours, Mitch and Carmen, visit me. Together with the owners of my favorite jewelry store, Bijou, they give me a beautiful Labradorite pendant I had been eyeing since the summer. Interesting how the meaning of Labradorite is to stimulate intuition, and can help you see through illusions and actualize your dreams and goals. What a timely gift! However, I know Louis's suggestion to leave it at home for safe keeping is probably the best even though I want to wear it every day.

----- Original Message -----
From: Louis Barre
Sent: Friday, October 15, 2004 10:49 PM
Subject: Carole Update — Day 17

Greetings everyone,

This week has been a busy one with me returning to work... can not just sit around and write emails in the middle of the night anymore!

The doctors still have not determined a cause for her stroke and, for the time being, they seem not to be doing further testing. She had a few more tests this past week, which ruled out several more possibilities but did not offer any further insight. So, she will continue to be on blood thinners to reduce the likelihood of future clotting problems.

As for visitors, Carole is now receiving them. In the interest of managing how many people come, and when, we ask that you call ahead to her cell phone. She can tell you when would be a good time and schedule you around rehab appointments and naps. Tomorrow, Carole will be on another leave-pass for the day so please do not stop by or you'll be disappointed to find she is not there.

As for the kids and me, we are doing well. We've enjoyed the ongoing support from parents/grandparents, neighbors, colleagues, friends and family, without which we could not have survived the past 18 days. As needed, we will continue to take advantage of the support available to us (... including some offers for meals when the time is right).

Thanks again for all your support, prayers and well wishes. They have been a significant contribution to Carole's recovery and have brought us great comfort during this difficult time.

In friendship and gratitude,
Louis

Tuesday, October 19, 2004

It's 6:30 in the morning and I'm awake. This is probably the best time to take a shower on my own for the first time. No nurse is in sight to stop me and everyone on the ward is still sleeping. This plan excites me because I'll avoid the patient line-ups outside the shower door so I'll be all by myself in these public showers. I feel like a child just accomplishing another big-person activity on my own for the first time. This feat deserves putting on makeup.

I have a second major milestone today. I can sit and toilet independently without using a toilet-commode that has armrests to keep me from falling. What new freedom and independence I never thought to appreciate! Of course, Chloé is thrilled I am now potty trained and proudly declares this to everyone.

Friday, October 22, 2004

This is a day for visitors from all the schools of the present. This morning, on behalf of my school, the chairperson of the parents' home and school council visits me bearing lovely gifts. Unfortunately, her timing is not the best. I can only briefly visit with her because I'm off to therapy. I feel guilty leaving so soon but therapy is on a tight schedule so as much as I worry about doing this, I want to trust she'll understand.

The poorly prepared hospital meals are not only bland but shockingly extremely low in nutrition. This forces me to indulge in visitors' invitations for any meal requests. I usually suggest a fresh salad. Today, with a professional development day for teachers and the students away from school, the secretaries where I work are coming to eat lunch with me. I can't wait to bite into their yummy salad they promised to bring and eat together. I miss my colleagues. My secretary friends brought me up to speed on the latest school news. I feel normal again.

Chloé has a day off from school and I can't wait to spend the afternoon with her. Late afternoon, Mme Manon, her grade two teacher, pleasantly surprises us with a visit while Chloé and I are playing dominoes. I had registered to attend a workshop presented by her teacher but given my circumstances, I obviously cannot attend. Mme Manon knows me well enough that I am so disappointed by this that she will come personally to share what I missed learning in her workshop today. She also gives me a report about Chloé's school progress and then we have a cheerful chat before she leaves. What dedication!

Chloé and I had a wonderful afternoon together and as much as I love her, I'm exhausted and can't wait to rest. I don't feel ready yet to engage socially for more than half an hour at a time. It's a lot for my brain, to listen, and to keep track of the conversation so I can interact accordingly. It can't seem to handle a lot at once. That is not me!

My roommates and I cannot wait for supper because Louis is bringing us sushi. I can't speak for my roommates but I know this is my big social event of the week. The ward staff is beginning to enjoy our Friday night takeout meals because they always get to eat the leftovers. We always make sure to order extra for them and to let them think they are eating our leftovers. What a bountiful day! Thank you Lord!

Sunday, October 24, 2004

I cannot help but feel continuously blessed. A fun couple from our group of church friends invited us all to their house for an outstanding brunch. They are always the perfect hosts and Annie as usual prepares the most delicious food. We had plenty of laughs and spent a pleasant afternoon together even though my first experience in learning how to maneuver a wheelchair inside a house took chunks of plaster out of their living room wall. Oops! So sorry.

Monday, October 25, 2004

----- Original Message -----
From: Louis Barre
Sent: Monday, October 25, 2004 1:27 AM
Subject: Carole Update – Day 27

Hi everyone,

As another weekend passes, I reflect upon the past few days. We have seen new progress, had Carole's first sleepover outside of the hospital, resumed some old routines, and had some difficult moments.

The week ahead will bring new accomplishments, new stories, new joys and perhaps even a few more tears. I find myself compelled to "share Carole's journey" as it seems to me that the richness of such an experience should not be wasted on just one family! And, without doubt, a large factor in Carole's recovery is the strength she draws from the support, well wishes and prayers she receives from family, friends, neighbors, and colleagues. She will continue to need the support and positive energy you bring to her, directly or indirectly, and for it she will be grateful.

Have a nice week!

Louis

----- Original Message -----
From: Louis Barre
Sent: Monday, October 25, 2004 9:30 PM
Subject: Carole Update — Day 27

Hey guys,

Me again. Good news and bad news today. Good news... Carole moved her thumb. Bad news... she feels like shopping again!

Tonight they had a Halloween dance party for the patients at Club Rehab. I must admit I am not much of a dancer and was more than a bit hesitant at first, but young men with two good legs were a hot commodity! When one lady in a wheelchair asked me if I was there with someone (pick-up line), I pointed out my beautiful wife and daughter and did not stop dancing with them until the last song ended!

Louis

Tuesday, October 26, 2004

Finally, my left leg is getting much stronger. I manage to walk up a flight of steps with only one person assisting me. What an accomplishment!

On another note, I am not so proud about laughing hysterically when a patient falls to the floor while trying to stand up on her own. I am upset about the whole incident but I'm confused because inside I am very worried she is hurt. However, all I that could come out of my mouth is hysterical laughter blocking any words of concern. Fortunately, the occupational therapist who first arrived on the scene explained to my roommate that my reaction is common with brain damage. Thankfully, my roommate has a good sense of humor and together we had belly laughs talking about the incident with our visitors and anyone willing to listen.

I am so spoiled: three girlfriends of mine from church, Amabelle, Chris and Judy take me out for dinner at a restaurant. They are determined not to let my stroke stop us from having our ritual of girls' night out dinners. Sitting in my wheelchair at the restaurant table, I wonder how many other people are out on a hospital pass like me pretending to be normal. I wish Louis would get breaks like this. He is working so hard in taking care of the family, keeping up with his work demands, and rushing to my every need that I worry he's not getting the rest he needs.

Thank goodness, my mom is here every day to help me in therapy—one less thing for Louis to have to do or worry about. Every day that my mom comes to see me makes for shorter and more pleasant days. She has been there for me every day with the exception of a few. Somehow, even though I know this is demanding of her time and energy, it is somehow good for both of us. In our many bouts of laughter, we have found a way to help each other cope with my new life circumstances.

Thursday, October 28, 2004

----- Original Message -----
From: Louis Barre
Sent: Thursday, October 28, 2004 11:48 PM
Subject: Carole update – Day 30

Hi everyone,

I feel like my emails must keep pace with Carole's progress and social life, which keeps me busy!

Carole was very excited today because she is now walking independently with a quad cane and they have allowed her to have the cane on the ward, which means she can walk about during the day and evening. Up until now, all her fancy footwork has been limited to her time in the gym and she was required to use the wheelchair everywhere else. They have entrusted her with this level of independence on the condition that she promise not to strike out on her own, and to walk only when she has another adult by her side, "just in case." Being the "rule observant" person she is, I got in trouble a couple of times today when I wandered more than a couple of feet from her side. I think she was afraid "she" would be caught breaking the rules and they'd take away her cane. It became quickly clear that she is not about to risk losing this newfound freedom and certainly not by any tawdry conduct on my part! Carole also joined the walking club yesterday, which enables her cover additional ground each day. Today, in total, she walked about 500 feet between her physio session, walking program, and trips to the bathroom.

For the first time, Carole was also able to move her big toe once yesterday, and twice today. With the exception of her upper leg, this is typical of the magnitude and pace of her recovery. When a movement returns, it is very small, and she can deliberately make the movement perhaps only one, two, or three times over a twenty-four hour period. "Speedy" (her arm) has made some modest improvement since last week. She can partially lift it off the bed about a dozen times per day. She can also slowly move her fingers and thumb toward a fist-like position a few times each day (still not enough to hold a credit card but she has the other hand for that!) One of the reasons Carole has been able to walk so well is that she wears a temporary splint to support her ankle while she walks. They don't know for how long she will need to wear the splint but for the time being it enables greater mobility and reduces the likelihood of injury, as her ankle is still otherwise quite unstable and wants to turn in. The good news is that the tightening of her ankle muscles may be a sign of more significant progress just around the corner.

Socially, Carole has not let any slow moving body parts hold her back. She was out for dinner with girlfriends twice this week and is planning to be on leave-pass this weekend as well. (We may just have to give her a curfew if her social life gets out of hand!) Wednesday night, accompanied by a dear girlfriend, she made a surprise visit home after dinner and greeted us at the front door of our house. We were excited to see her and hosted her like a guest in her own home. It was fun for all of us and she got to leave without doing dishes! She was also able to tuck Chloé into bed, which was a real treat for both of them.

Tomorrow, one of Carole's four roommates will be leaving the hospital -- going home after many weeks. Everyone will be sad to see her go. A bond develops between the patients, especially those who share the same limited space for eating, sleeping and other of nature's processes! When the patients first arrive on the ward, I think they may not be too excited about having four people in one room. But, it quickly becomes apparent that despite any one person's quirkiness, the social interactions and friendships that ensue are important contributing factors to their recovery. And, if one patient does not get many visitors, they can enjoy the social spill-over from their roommates. Carole's roommates have also been able to enjoy a wide variety of flowers, snacks, drinks, chocolates, and other treats. They always seem surprised at just what she has stored in that little cupboard by her bedside and the variety of her offerings. Tonight she was able to offer two kinds of cookies, five kinds of chocolates and three kinds of specialty teas after they finished the Chinese food one of them ordered in for the group.

It has now been just over four weeks since Carole had her stroke and the Rehab staff is already planning for her return home. They expect she will be discharged in about three weeks and for Carole, it feels too soon. Next week, we will have a home assessment to determine what changes we need to make to the house. I expect it will mostly involve handrails along stairways. Carole has a vision for some "decorative handrail" for the main staircase: something with a "designer touch" that I expect we will not be able to find at Home Depot!

If you plan to visit Carole, I suggest that you call her on her cell phone ahead of time. This is the best way to ensure you will find her there to receive your visit. Please also feel free to call her to say hi. She enjoys brief phone calls and does her best to return messages.

Have a nice weekend!

Louis

Monday, November 8, 2004

----- Original Message -----
From: Louis Barre
Sent: Monday, November 08, 2004 2:33 AM
Subject: Carole Update -- Day 40

Greetings everyone,

As a good Catholic I feel compelled to begin this email with, "Forgive me Father for I have sinned. It has been 10 days since I sent my last Carole Update." With the usual pace of family life and added routines surrounding Carole and the hospital, time has passed quickly. Despite this, ten days seems like ten months. And I would characterize these ten days as the days "reality and exhaustion set in."

Chloe also "hit the wall" this week. After more than a month of tending to her mom's every need with absolute enthusiasm and dedication, she no longer necessarily wants to be part of every bath or dressing routine, or to run and fetch those items that always happen to be in the other room. She too has needed a break. As for me, I have come down with a nasty cold. Thankfully, Carole and I have wonderfully supportive parents and family who truly have been here for us. And friends and neighbors continue to avail themselves to our needs.

Carole has spent the last two weekends at home with us, returning to the hospital on Sunday evening. Transitioning back home has meant new firsts and new feelings. While home, Carole spends much of her time resting and much of the remainder of her time finding new ways to do old things, such as climbing steps, bathing, getting dressed, performing one handed hair-do's, holding a book and turning pages, and making breakfast. With one arm and one good leg, the most basic activities can be challenging if not seemingly impossible and always time consuming. (A big accomplishment this week was reducing the time to put on her bra from ten minutes to one minute, without pulling it into pieces in the process.) It has often felt like the object or task is too far, too high, too small, too heavy, or just plain too hard and too much! Thankfully, Carole's occupational therapist has taught her some techniques to make life easier and empower her. For example, at "breakfast class" last week, she learned how to butter bread with one hand. And once she has the special cutting board and knife, meant for one-handed people, she expects to be able to slice vegetables with safety and precision. Despite the many frustrations and to her credit, Carole has persisted with determination to relearn these basic tasks. It would be easier to just give up or let others do it for her but this hasn't been Carole's approach.

On a cheery note, Carole and her two roommates, who now call themselves the three musketeers, have developed the reputation for being the party room on their floor. They order in food at least once per week, which they share with staff, and they chat and laugh a lot. All of them have experienced their shares of hardship but are now feeling well enough to enjoy one another's company. If they were three men, I am sure they may barely know one another's name after just one month, but as women stricken by adversity and stuck in a room together, they have become lasting soul-mates!

As I mentioned in my last email, the fourth roommate (also a young woman) left about ten days ago. Earlier last week, a new roommate arrived -- a young "man" who could walk and talk! It was quite the stir to have a young fellow amongst the girls. At first they weren't quite sure if this was a good idea but having shared the women's bathroom with the men on the ward for the past month (the women's bathroom is being repaired), it did not take them too long to get past any initial reluctance and grow fond of the new company! They could always pull the curtains when necessary! This evening when I returned Carole to the hospital, one of the other women was also returning from her weekend pass. To their surprise and disappointment their new "male" roommate had been transferred to another room with men. There was collective concern and comments to the effects of, "I think it would be better for him if they left him in here with us!" and "Oh, I suppose they are now going to put another woman in here with us. She better be interesting!" My sense is that they think it was a pretty dirty trick to give them a man for three or four days and then take him away with no forewarning the minute they had their backs turned!

We are not sure what the next 10 days will bring but we do know that in 12 days Carole expects to be discharged home -- on Friday, November 19th. She is feeling a bit anxious about this. It is one thing to come home for a day or two days over the weekend when there is a house full of mostly eager family members at her beck and call, but being discharged home means she won't be able to return to the security of hospital where everything is set up to support her for the other five days of the week. It also means she won't have the daily occupational and physiotherapy sessions which represent a lifeline to her recovery process. Unfortunately, there is a 4-8 week waiting period for outpatient rehab, which means she won't likely resume formal therapy at the hospital until after Christmas. Even then, she expects to have only two outpatient sessions per week. As a result, we are pursuing other possibilities and are lucky to have some options in the interim.

Thank you for your continued support.

I look forward to a week of new possibilities.

Louis

----- Original Message -----
From: Louis Barre
Sent: Friday, November 19, 2004 12:57 AM
Subject: Carole Update - Day 51

Hi everyone,

Just a quick note to report that Carole's discharge from the hospital has been delayed. She was expecting to be released tomorrow but, on the advice of her doctor, she has decided to wait until she has home care in place. We are not sure how long this will take. Initially, we thought she could manage at home without home care but have decided that it will be best for her if she has some personal support each morning as the kids and I are off to school and work very early. Given enough time, she is now capable of managing steps and completing most personal routines independently. However, it will be safer and less frustrating to have a little bit of assistance. We would hate to have her fall and experience a set-back. The added benefit of a delayed discharge is that she will continue with her in-patient rehab for a longer period.

As for her recovery, she is doing pretty well. She is now practicing walking with a regular cane (versus the quad, a four legged cane) and she can even take a few short steps without her cane (in rehab). Her leg is slowly gaining more strength and her balance is improving but her knee, and particularly her ankle, are still not too stable. The therapists may fit her for a leg brace to provide additional support. Her arm and hand continue to progress very slowly so they aren't yet of much use. She has had some ongoing problems and tenderness in her shoulder and wrist so she treats them with care to avoid pain and further problems. Unfortunately, this impedes her rehab but for the time being there is not much more that can be done.

As Carole's time in the hospital is nearing an end, it has begun to feel like the last few days at summer camp. She is packing up her belongings including the many gifts and cards she received, savoring the company of last meals shared together, and exchanging phone numbers. By this Friday, all of her buddy-roommates will have been discharged and the energy level of the room will be very different. It will not be quite the same when the three musketeers aren't together! But, they are committed to reconnecting once again, probably in the spring when the weather is friendly. By then, they all hope to be physically much better and will likely fondly reminisce about the significant moments they shared together at "Club Rehab."

So much for a quick email! By now, I should know better than to sit down before this computer at such a late hour. Time quickly slides by and before I know it, I have committed myself to yet another sleepy day behind my desk! Maintaining adequate rest continues to be my biggest challenge.

I hope this email finds you well and enjoying the last few days of wonderful weather before winter sets in and Christmas is upon us!

With gratitude,
Louis

Friday, November 19, 2004

Today, while I'm in my physiotherapy session, the discharge nurse informs me I can have home care service starting Monday if I they discharge me today. This is too much information to make sense of so the eager-to-please beaver in me agrees to go home. Soon after the discharge nurse walks away, my therapist runs off to assist another patient in his exercise session, which seems to be for a long time. In hindsight, I had unwisely agreed to be discharged because I was unaware of how I lost my ability to make well-informed decisions on impulse, and therefore not able to quickly think through the consequences.

Left alone with this overwhelming news, the questions of how I will live as a hemiplegic in the real world suddenly consume me. Oh my God! Why didn't I know I'm not emotionally prepared for this next phase? This revelation terrifies me so much that intense emotions erupt beyond my control: I cry non-stop with streams of tears and no tissues. I try suppressing the tears but they end up rolling out uncontrollably into hysterical laughter like aimless flooding waters. Then, in a flash, I revert to uncontrollable crying once again. People in the gymnasium must think I am crazy. My emotional behavior is out of my control. The staff seems unconcerned and my attending therapist, who usually is very attentive, is preoccupied with another patient. She eventually returns and upset by my emotional state tries to comfort me before sending me back to my ward. She too feels helpless and all she can do is send me along with tissues in hand. All day, as I wait for Louis to arrive, I struggle to hold back the tears and sometimes find myself at the losing end of this internal tug-of-war.

I leave the hospital in my wheelchair, with a quad cane and a regular cane in tow. My gear supposedly is here to help me face the battle of learning how to live and cope with physical disabilities. I imagine this might be what a soldier feels like. Wheeled off with his battle gear, not knowing what to expect and how it will truly help him to face what is ahead, and how will this stuff make up for what is lost.

All the way home in the van, I sob incessantly in the presence of a quiet husband and daughter, both not knowing what to say to comfort me. I continue to cry during a lovely supper prepared by our cousin, Michelle, visiting from California and here just for me and us. I now feel worse because I think I have ruined her dinner and my home-coming for everyone. I am even more upset with myself and sob profusely once more.

Monday, November 22, 2004

----- Original Message -----
From: Louis Barre
Sent: Monday, November 22, 2004 11:50 PM
Subject: Carole Update - Day 55

Greetings!

Carole is now home to stay. She was discharged last Friday afternoon after all. We had expected there would be some delays due to the need for home care but they were able to arrange it on short notice.

Leaving the hospital was a bit difficult for Carole as, at some level, she had expected she would be farther in her recovery process than she is at this point. However, after a few short days, she is adjusting well to new routines and we are all glad to have some new life around the house. I do not think we realized how much we missed her until she was back! She is learning some more one-handed tricks and finding that her teeth are useful for more things than chewing food!

Louis

Monday, December 6, 2004

----- Original Message -----
From: Louis Barre
Sent: Monday, December 06, 2004 1:11 AM
Subject: Carole Update - Day 67

Hi everyone,

It has been about two weeks since Carole left the hospital but somehow that seems like a very long time ago. This period has been marked by a mixture of emotions, hard work and some good progress.

At a physical level, Carole is working intensely hard on her rehabilitation. She is fortunate to have a wonderful physiotherapist (and friend), Mary, who comes to our home three times per week to do therapy. We have set up a portion of the living room for rehab, with a therapy table and exercise bike. Each day, Carole does a minimum of one hour (usually more) of rigorous exercises to rebuild the strength and movement in her leg, arm and hand. Despite her weak ankle, and very awkward appearing gait, her ability to walk has improved tremendously, as have her stamina and balance. For the past few days, Carole has mostly abandoned her wheelchair and we have even ventured into Winnipeg's winter without it. On the weekend, we were able to go to church, walk up and down basement stairs, twice, and carefully maneuver long, icy sidewalks, all without the wheelchair. Tackling the icy sidewalks may not have been the best idea but she did it! This was a very significant milestone and Carole felt great about it.

"Speedy," Carole's arm, has some serious catching up to do. Despite rigorous daily exercises, her hand and arm have regained some movement but relatively very little. This pace of recovery is typical for most stroke victims. Each day Carole tracks her exercise and progress and, much of the time, progress in parts of her hand is measured in "flickers" in her muscles, not major movements. And even these minor movements require her to concentrate intensely and leave her feeling exhausted as if she had just lifted heavy weights. Part of the struggle with her arm is also the pain she was experiencing in her shoulder, in fact, both shoulders. Accidental movement in her bad shoulder can send her screaming with pain. And even her good shoulder is suffering some problems from over-use, pulling, pushing, and twisting in unfamiliar ways in its effort to compensate. Carole's hand and shoulder problems are not unique; rather, apparently, common to stroke victims. Nonetheless, they are frustrating. I can easily understand how many people give up on trying to regain use of their arm and hand. It is plainly and simply hard work that does not seem to reward much. And it is much easier to climb back on the couch and have another nap! Despite this, Carole continues to persevere and, together, we are able to laugh at the funny faces she makes in her effort to accomplish those very little movements. Thankfully, she has a good sense of humor about these particular difficulties and has even been willing to liven up a dull gathering on a couple of occasions.

One of the other significant outcomes of the stroke was the paralysis and numbing of Carole's facial muscles. The paralysis now seems mostly corrected but the numbness, or sense of being frozen like following dental work, persisted for a long time. For more than two months, Carole's face felt like she had just been at the dentist's office. However, one day last week, a significant area of numbness in her face lifted and she is now left with tingling around the left side of her mouth and tip of her tongue only. The stroke also affected Carole's ability to taste properly. Everything continues to taste salty and almost nothing tastes very satisfying, except some very expensive chocolates! Hmmm. Go figure!

Since Carole's return home, Chloe has begun to process the experience at a different level. She asked her mom if kids can have strokes and if she will one day have one because her mom has? And she does not want her school friends to see her mom because "nobody else at school has a mom like hers." These were difficult words for Carole to hear but they were shared by Chloé in honesty and innocence and because she felt safe to do so. And, we remind ourselves that she is only six, a fact easily overlooked because of her commitment to caring for her mom and willingness to help-out around the house.

We continue to be indebted to the many people who have helped us in tangible and intangible ways. Family, friends, neighbors and colleagues have been wonderful. We have had many meals delivered, and help with housework, driving kids, Christmas shopping, wrapping, and baking. I know that this journey Carole is taking us on will continue for some time. But, we are very hopeful and I can not help but feel that there will be many more good than bad days ahead of us. And we will continue to draw from the positive energy you bring us, each in your own ways. Thank you for being here for us.

Louis

What Doesn't Kill You Strengthens You

God didn't promise days without pain, laughter without sorrow, or sun without rain, but He did promise strength for the day, comfort for the tears, and light for the way. If God brings you to it, He will bring you through it.—Anonymous

My strokes could have physically killed me, but they did not. Like all other life-changing challenges, this one strengthened me. It was no stroke of luck that I survived. It was by the grace of God and my desire to fulfill my sacred contract.

Many times when I found myself at crossroads in life, I avoided making choices because of the fear of the unknown. Facing, and venturing into, the uncertainty of the unknown would have required courage, risk-taking, faith, and self-trust. I feared there would be hidden albatrosses, failures, and more pain and suffering, possibly worse than I was experiencing. I was sometimes certain that I couldn't take on any more burdens than what I was already managing. When I let these fears paralyze me from taking risks and exploring uncharted territories, I chose the paths of least resistance with familiar, predictable discomforts and pains I knew from experience I could control.

Recovering from a stroke challenged me to practice risk-taking. There were many paths to choose from—like shopping avenues lined with window fronts inviting me to come in and try new ways of living life. I only had the currency of blind faith and with that, and my imagination, I assumed faith in myself and in God were the risks with the most potential yields. I visualized storefronts filled with my doing the physical activities I had set as goals, from baby steps to walking without walking aids. I imagined I could buy these with a huge leap of faith and that I would eventually accomplish the countless little movements for the big goals of walking independently and getting reasonable functional use of my arm.

This did not mean I wore rose-colored glasses as one of my early physiotherapists once insinuated of me when I shared with her my long-term goals. Contrary to what she believed, I was truly honest with myself about my physical status, no matter how devastatingly painful this was to face. Despite the permanent neurological damage, and my hemiplegia, I knew the road ahead was going to be arduous and held no guarantees. I've passed my ninth year stroke anniversary and even though my hemiparesis is barely noticeable, I still have invisible disabilities and, as time passes, the lingering deficits are becoming more manageable.

Every time I accomplished a physical movement, even a minute muscle twitch, my faith in achieving good recovery increased and I felt more capable of getting past this painful experience. I also found the emotional and physical strength to work even harder. Never giving up on physical therapy and having hope was paid off by increased faith and strength to continue going onward. Taking the risk of investing in hope and blind faith did not kill me, but strengthened me. It gave me strength to smile, to think positive and to appreciate being alive.

By the grace of God I was blessed with the ability to see those gifts and to have a positive attitude.

Active and Passive Choices

When dealing with adversity, there are two possible choices. Passive choices are those to which I give away my power in shaping the outcomes. This is disempowering. Active choices are those for which I do my best to determine the outcomes. This is empowering.

The fear of the unknown can paralyze a person into not taking action through risk-taking so consequently miss out on discovering its hidden treasures. It can also entail a lack of perseverance or a commitment to achieve better outcomes and thus increase the chance of failure. The passive choices are discouraging because the outcomes don't generate feelings of accomplishment and satisfaction. They can sometimes even stifle healthy growth psychologically, physically, or spiritually. Passive choices are like giving up and saying they are too difficult. For example, to forgive someone, to learn how to walk, or to generate new brain pathways to move an arm again.

Passive choices would have kept me imprisoned in the present life-challenge to make me forget it was a temporary situation, one without hope for better, future outcomes. Giving up on functional physical recovery would have meant succumbing to living life in a wheelchair and accepting that I could do no better than be dependent on others for most things. It would have felt like sitting in a waiting room next to death's door. I wasn't willing to do this. Essentially, giving up would have been letting go of any possibility of having a meaningful life.

I learned and still believe it is easier to accept the situation as is and that this too shall pass. Although I had no idea how much of my paralysis would go away, I chose to believe it would certainly get better. This kind of thinking continues to inspire me to never give up.

I purposefully adopt positive thought patterns with the desired outcome in mind. I learned from several inspirational speakers that it is important to visualize a desired outcome by feeling and imagining it with all my senses as though I am already living it. In other words, to own it as it is already happening. Using my imagination to picture my senses experiencing what I want or where I want to be as though were in the present moment. This helps me feel I'm already there even though this is only in my mind. I imagine the smells and tastes of the food I cook using my left hand, the feeling of freedom when I wear any shoes without an AFO (ankle foot orthotic), the feeling of walking like a goddess when I wear pretty shoes, hearing the accolades of observers marveling at how well I walk without the AFO and cane. This valuable process of visualization is now one of my many approaches I use today for all other goals.

Visualization relates to the law of attraction: like attracts like. For example, people who think alike are drawn to each other. It makes sense to me why thoughts influence us. If I think I'm unworthy, I will attract people who reinforce that I am unworthy. That is why I focus on healthy thoughts, it's to attract into my life positive outcomes and positive people with healthy energy. Thoughts set the stage for where I want to be and visualization with an action plan—in mind or written down—is a good start to get there. Making active choices involves patience, determination, action, commitment, and perseverance to discover the life-changing choices born out of adversities.

Most of us have known at least one life-altering experience where, in the end, we came out a stronger person with new insights, skills and other unexpected benefits. Even if only one thing in us changed for the better then it is cause for celebration. Difficult situations force us to make choices that create opportunities for us to grow. They can be catalysts for growth if we let them.

Helpful insights about living life fully arise from making active choices. They are life-giving. Undoubtedly, active choices do not mean these paths are paved smoothly. Most anything worthwhile requires hard work and dedication. For example, through surviving a difficult divorce in my early thirties I learned that the power was in my hands to make desirable changes in my life. This, as well as my happiness, are my responsibilities and are dependent on me and on no one else. Who says we have to spend the rest of our lives with the cards we're dealt? I remember someone in a writer's workshop once telling me: "It's not the cards you're dealt. It's how you play the game."

Metaphorically, whenever I figured I was headed for a cliff, and every time I took command of the driver's wheel by making active choices, I steered my life to safe places where I could park for a while. The cliff, so to speak, didn't kill me but was an opportunity to show me a life-giving place to go to. Challenges are meant to motivate change and to strengthen us. They can literally or metaphorically kill us if we let them by our own acts of giving in to complacency for instant gratification.

Overcoming Why Me? Why This? Why Now?

It is not whether you get knocked down. It is whether you get up again.—Vince Lombardi

September 29, 2004, provoked new fears and panic that replaced the old fears I had resolved in August. I had worked too hard to get where I was spiritually and physically to give up the peace I had found since my quest to outwit my date with destiny. I would be damned if I was going to give up now even though the stroke inconvenienced the lives of my family and friends—not to mention, mine. Despite all my well-intended efforts to not have self-pity, I had many whys that tormented me.

Why Me?

There were no healthy answers to this question that could immediately satisfy me so I gave up looking for answers. Certainly, the temptation to feel punished crossed my mind when I awoke half-paralyzed. I knew this question would only deepen my sense of sadness and loss. So my next question was, "Have I not been a good

Christian? Do my efforts to remain connected with You not count?" It is so easy to ask these questions when facing a crisis and assuming you've been forsaken. Since my stroke, I've learned how futile it can be to ask these questions.

Every time I face extremely difficult events, my gut wants me to ask, why me. For example, "Why me?" made its fleeting appearance when a close family member made a choice that led along a painful life-changing path. Asking why me adds to that sense of helplessness, that things happen just to hurt me.

Even in my half-paralyzed state, I soon realized that focusing on why me generated intense, negative thoughts and emotions that affected my psyche. This, in turn, brewed an unhealthy mental attitude. I decided to stop asking why me and to believe that God was not punishing me. This new thought pattern helped me see that I could either grow from this experience or continue to view myself as a victim. Growth seemed more appealing. It occurred to me that I should perhaps be asking a different question: "What can I learn from this?"

While in the rehab hospital, this epiphany inspired me to think of childhood mentors. How lucky was I to have my mémère Laurin and her mother, Dina, my mémère Emond, to have taught me about faith and strength of character. When I was 8 years old, my mémère Emond died but in the few years we had together she had left a lasting impact. She had inspired me with her many gems about living with faith. Mémère Laurin continued the same legacy of living with faith. My maternal mentors ignited my desire for a solid, personal relationship with God, Jesus, the saints and the angels.

Their advice: God only gives us what we can handle, and prayers manifest in the presence of full faith and in the absence of all doubt. Those two wise statements always encourage me and remind me to be patient during life challenges. It wasn't until my paralyzing stroke that I finally learned how to practice those beliefs successfully.

How does one let go of all anxieties, and the worries tied to wanting our prayers and requests answered as desired? I began with thinking about my mémères' two influential teachings. Although my mémères taught me simply to give all doubts and fears to God and to believe he'd take care of me, they hadn't taught me practical, concrete ways to accomplish this.

When I was dealing with my reactions to the paralysis, all I wanted was to lie there waiting for God to help me. I couldn't get up and go places to distract me from what was plaguing my body. Despite the prescribed, stroke-related antidepressants, I thought I'd go crazy with this helplessness. I needed to learn how to truly trust in God. Therefore, I politely—and trustingly—assigned God the task of providing me with what or with whom I needed to overcome my hurdles.

Gradually, with blind faith—and time—I learned that prayers get answered and life's burdens get lifted, but in God's way and fashion. Somehow, things always seemed to fall into place at the right time. Whenever my process became too burdensome, I learned that asking God and his helpers to carry me through it, helped with the healing.

Another thing I learned since my stroke, is that one big trauma like a paralyzing stroke did not immunize my life from subsequent traumas or major disappointments. Nor did it guarantee that my tab of Life's Bad Things To Happen had been paid in full, or that the rest of my life was going to be pain free. Although it might feel for some of us that we have had more of life's share in disappointment and pain, life is that. Life is really about learning how to roll with the punches, it can taste sweet or sour depending on how we flavor them. Bad things happen. Bad things are not meant to maim us but to heal, strengthen, deepen our faith and teach us how to live life better and more fully.

For example, in the hospital bed I decided the stroke, as big and scary as it seemed, must be, at its most, a challenge for me and at its least, a challenge for my family to grow and to learn about ourselves and each other. Somehow, this belief had brought me peace and stopped me from asking: Why me?

But there was no lasting peace because the next question, "Why this?" began to preoccupy my thoughts.

Why This?

Throughout past crises when asking God why this, I had realized that what I was really asking was: Why do I have to learn life's lessons through such pain, suffering and/or loss. Isn't there an easier way?

Why a stroke? Why this? Could this be a lesson for my spiritual journey? If so, why does it have to be as severe as hemiplegia? Asking these kinds of questions made me think I had been given a harsh lesson. In my pursuit to answer these questions, I became bitter and angry. Harping on the question "why this" had obviously been hurtful and not helpful, so I thought of another question, "How can I benefit from this?"

First, I acknowledged that my stroke was a major calling card. Then my answer came: this whole experience was a catalyst for me to learn, to grow and then to share what I learned—and I had to embrace it. But the next question popped up, "How do I do this?" I could think of only two choices: have an attitude of pessimism or of optimism. Pessimism would intensify my loss, pain, resentment, anger, and reaffirm that my stroke had been a punishment or a curse. Therefore, pessimism was not an option.

I recalled that previous experiences of having an optimistic attitude had given me hope and had led to good outcomes. This was my best option. A positive attitude would serve me better toward coping with my hemiplegia and with making the best of my recovery. A happy attitude would ease my journey. I needed patience and this seemed the most promising way of getting it.

How did I find the power to heal this and survive subsequent adversities? I had to accept my fears and face them. I found solace and strength in silent meditation and prayer which chased away negative thoughts and images. Only then, could I adopt positive thoughts and consequently acquire the courage to deal with recovery and subsequent adversities.

Whether it is stroke recovery or a family crisis, my first instinct was always to wish it away. Then, as in the case of my stroke, I wished for a miracle, for a medical treatment that would restore me to full mobility. However, as the weeks passed, the flaccid half of my body made it clear that I would be dealing with this alone. No one could experience this journey but me. They could only walk alongside me. I've since observed this is also true for any life challenge even if an event affects others along with me. We all cope differently with stress. How we choose to cope determines if we are in control or are powerless, and that is the solo part of our journeys.

It deeply saddened me that it was all up to me to survive this physical and spiritual journey. Could I develop the motivation, the inner strength, the faith in God to see this ordeal to the end? This fear motivated me to invite God, the angels and saints, and any divine beings out there to come to my aid and accompany me. Even though in the beginning I didn't feel any presence but my own, I forced myself to believe they were there. Holding on tightly to that belief helped me find comfort and peace and to experience the company of God and his divine beings as I faced the deep, dark halls of poststroke depression.

I had to work at not being afraid to sit alone in silence. Walking alone in my soul meant taking time for being quiet, to meditate. This could not happen until I stopped entertaining my worries, anxieties, and negative conversations and experiences. Silencing my mind post stroke allowed me to reconnect with my inner voice where I found thoughts that gave me the strength to go on. When my inner voice couldn't drown out the negative and pessimistic thoughts, I asked

God while I meditated to take care of them. I believed He would. My mémères would have advised me to do it that way. Meditation and faith somehow made me receptive to opportunities for recovery and self-growth. Positive thinking became easier and my inner voice louder. Giving to God what I couldn't handle had worked! When I quieted my mind enough through silence, meditation and prayer, I had rediscovered my divine, inner voice. This voice slowly and strongly guides me to use the qualities of my soul to be true to who I am. I also learned that being truthful about my fears, and having faith, practicing meditation, and having a positive attitude and optimistic thoughts, attract opportunities for growth and success.

The above approach to meditation did not become clear until years later when I heard Dr. Deepak Chopra on *The Dr. Oz Show*. He stated how positive thoughts alone are ineffective. He further explained that to be receptive for positivity one must get rid of emotional toxins through meditation, which clears the mind and enables one to hear one's inner voice.

Why Now?

I was baffled as was everyone else close to me about why my healthy lifestyle had not prevented my stroke. In the weeks prior to my stroke, I had begun a renewed routine of prayer and meditation and was experiencing a new level of spiritual consciousness. Why had this not mattered to God? I asked myself. "Why now?" evoked confusion and anger in me. The timing of the stroke was illogical. I was in disbelief that taking good care of my body and soul had not been enough, especially since, at the time of my stroke, I felt whole and well! This renewed spiritual practice of mine insured a healthy body, mind, and soul. Did it not?

Lying in a hospital bed for nearly two months afforded me the time to think about "Why now?" I soon realized that it was not about timing but that I doubted God. I could not understand how hemiplegia could possibly be good for my family and me. I would not accept this. Once again, my faith was tested.

I wanted reassurance that my life would be meaningful and worth living despite the stroke. There were no guarantees and as difficult as this is to believe, I decided to interpret my stroke as a divine act. Adopting the belief that God was there with me along the entire way became less illogical as I experienced successes in stroke recovery. Incidentally, in other subsequent adversities, I had no problem knowing I had God there to carry me if I couldn't walk the rest of any challenging or painful journey.

Having faith and trusting in my inner voice became easier. It became second nature. For me, faith means letting go of having to know what will be, freedom from the need to understand the whys of everything. This is the reason I now always say, "It is what it is!" meaning: "I have no control of the outside world and others, only the control of how I interpret them. I know the whys don't change anything and the questions worth answering are those that determine how I react and cope with adversity."

I did indeed at first feel God had given me a disabled body with which to navigate my soul's journey. To be honest, I saw it as an inadequate vehicle. Nevertheless, I was alive—in a manner of speaking—and chose to stay in the driver's seat of my life. In the end, it doesn't matter that I'm not a Rolls-Royce or a used vehicle. My soul's inner voice is my GPS and directs me to self-actualize the best I can be and to where I must be.

An inspirational teacher once told me that when someone is in tune with one's soul, one can encounter distractions—challenges—on one's spiritual path. When this occurs, it does not mean we are failing as spiritual beings but that the lessons are necessary for our spiritual growth. What an encouraging way to answer our whys.

Overcoming Self Pity, Bitterness, and Resentment

Experience has taught me all too well that self-pity traps me in bitter and resentful thoughts. To avoid this, I thought that seeking and expressing gratitude whenever and however possible would avert this. Shifting my thoughts to gratitude since the stroke prompted me to abandon the questions, "Why me?" "Why This?" "Why now?"

My new guiding questions for all life challenges are, "For what or whom can I be thankful?" "How can I grow from this?" and "How shall I choose to react?" Diagram A below, "The Whys of Why Not," visually presents this.

The question, "For what or whom can I be thankful?" influenced me to not expect a big miracle. Instead, it opened the door to joy and to being as grateful for the small things in life as for the less numerous, grander ones. This question helps focus on the now, not on the what might be.

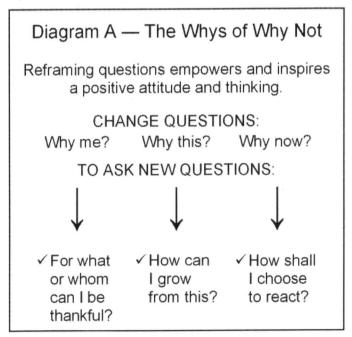

Diagram A — The Whys of Why Not

Reframing questions empowers and inspires a positive attitude and thinking.

CHANGE QUESTIONS:
Why me?   Why this?   Why now?

TO ASK NEW QUESTIONS:

↓   ↓   ↓

✓ For what or whom can I be thankful?   ✓ How can I grow from this?   ✓ How shall I choose to react?

Answering this new question generated and increased my gratitude in countless ways. Most gestures and events I once had taken for granted became increasingly apparent as parts of answered prayers. I saw these kind acts as God helping me through them. For instance, the bird perched outside my window chirping the entire time I sat in my chair, was reminding me that I wasn't alone. Whether that was true or not didn't matter. What helped was believing that God was with me. The more gratitude I chose to have, the easier it was for me to be receptive to God and His universe's gifts of loving kindness and support.

Maintaining gratitude and a positive attitude amid adversity is not without lapses into self-pity and other pitfalls. The physical challenges I faced were a large cross to bear despite how they became manageable over time. Immediately after the stroke, it did not take long to discover that I had physically regressed to what seemed to be a helpless toddler. My mother, my husband, and my daughter were now helping me with toileting and dressing. That I'd lost the ability to do these tasks for myself deeply saddened me and gave me a taste of what many people eventually experience in old age.

Facing the many physical losses all at once was daunting. Initially, my body was too exhausted from the stroke trauma to comprehend and absorb the impact of its devastation. Brain damage assisted in this delay because the strokes affected my capacity to process thoughts and emotions. It was not until a couple of weeks after my strokes that I was emotionally able to recognize, admit to, and *process* why I felt like a train wreck.

Before I could take my first step, I had to strengthen my core muscles. I had to relearn how to sit up without rolling over like Humpty Dumpty falling off his wall. I also had to relearn how to move the muscles in my left leg and hip so I could stand. I was astonished at how much concentration was required to orchestrate and consciously command every single muscle involved in taking just one step. Literally learning to walk all over again one step at a time, forced me to live life one day at a time. For that, I am grateful.

"How can I grow from this?" I knew that this and any other life challenge could either make me or break me. The saying, "What doesn't kill you strengthens you" is true, but what I discovered was that it's not the event that strengthens you, it's how you respond to it. Listening to my inner voice has always pointed me toward healthy thinking, and living.

I cannot help but believe there were divine reasons for my stroke. One of them was to divert my busy, distracting life toward my life's purpose. Juggling the increasing demands of work, home and the community invited unhealthy stress. Managing these obligations prevented me from living my soul's mission. The stroke somehow ensured that I discontinue these unhealthy patterns.

"How shall I choose to react?" forced me to focus on action and less on expectation. Taking responsibility for my recovery was the first way of empowering me when there had been so much loss. The next step was to accept the help of willing therapists toward the best physical recovery.

All I had were my thoughts and beliefs. Remembering the passage "God helps those who help themselves" inspired me to also ask, "What must I do?" So, I built an armor of healthy thoughts and leaned on the crutches of hope that my soul's infinite wisdom would eventually guide me to find strength, perseverance, and courage. The rest was up to God and Me.

My physical impairments would have been enough reason to feel justified in being angry, resentful, bitter, and to wallow in self-pity. For example, my left arm, locked in a ninety-degree angle, and my fisted hand were incapable of movement. No matter how I willed my brain, it could not loosen nor straighten the muscles in my arm and crippled fingers. However, the determination to work those fingers again, and understanding the value of positive thinking and gratitude, helped me persist. As difficult as this often was, and still can be, it is the only road for me.

What Next?

Since the stroke, I experienced countless blessings and new exciting opportunities such as this book and speaking engagements. I have also met wonderful people placed on my path to assist me in achieving my life's purpose. Truly blessed I am to have the love, support and caring of family, friends, colleagues, the church community and acquaintances. It would have been difficult to see all these blessings if I had remained stuck on the first three questions finding answers only in bitterness, resentment and anger.

In doing my research for the writing of this book, I developed an understanding of how thoughts and words have powerful energy. The book *Hidden Messages in Water*, written by Masaru Emoto proves this in such a concrete way through his experiments with frozen water crystals. He discovered that negative words distorted water crystals. One can conclude that negative words have the power not only to be emotionally hurtful but to be physically hurtful.

Negative words attract negative energy. Instinctively, I knew that negative words and thoughts affected my emotional well-being such as feeling that I was not worthy. This caused me to be full of self-doubt. It is fascinating how these concepts are now talked about on TV talk shows like *Oprah*.

Whenever I allowed myself to walk down a path of negative thoughts, I became emotionally vulnerable to the related negative energies they attracted. For example, I would attract encounters with other patients in therapy sessions who were none too happy to focus on the woes of their physical ailments. If I engaged in these conversations, I found I began to think in similar fashion and walked away not uplifted but discouraged and full of self-pity. Recognizing this, I deliberately avoided places, people, beliefs, and words that attracted negative thoughts and energy until I was strong enough not to be affected by it. I needed to pray, meditate, verbally express positive thoughts as much as possible to remain grounded and in a healthy state of mind

Life is much better when I cut out needless worries and meaningless tasks. Giving attention—my energy—to fears and doubts was unproductive. I needed to slow down my racing mind by stopping wasteful worrying and as Rick Warren describes in his book, *The Purpose Driven Life*, avoid focusing on aimless distractions.

I was determined to respond to the stress of stroke with calmness, new ears and eyes. Prior to the stroke, I had the habit of seeing almost every inconvenience in life as a "problem." I have since learned that upsetting events are inconveniences and very few are real problems. Breaking a valued object is an inconvenience, whereas having a stroke is a veritable problem worthy of my time and attention. By not viewing the stroke as a curse, I opened my mind to a new perspective on how to view a problem. The stroke presented a real problem and I chose to accept this as an opportunity to discover and reveal strengths in myself, not think of myself as having been cursed by some outside force.

Consequently, when I stay grounded through meditation and prayer, stressful events are manageable, and living in positive thoughts is achievable. I feel less burdened. I can then knowingly and willingly respond calmly and with love to most events without wasting precious energy.

Any fact facing us is not as important as our attitude toward it, for that determines our success or failure. The way you think about a fact may defeat you before you ever do anything about it. You are overcome by the fact because you think you are.
—Norman Vincent Peale

Faith in God (a Higher Power) and Self-Trust

Faith is to believe what you do not see; the reward of this faith is to see what you believe.—St Augustine

The years of intensive stroke recovery became an excellent training ground to learn new coping strategies and to live in the now, to not worry about what is yet to come. A healthy mindset, attitude, behaviors, and spiritual practices manifest in positive stroke recovery and most of all, in all subsequent life challenges.

Several years after my stroke, life threw my family and me more major curve balls. Instead of thinking I had enough on my plate, I chose to see these as opportunities to put into practice all the coping strategies learned during stroke recovery. As I knew deep down, they helped my family and me ride the tides of our challenges.

I learned that having faith is not about giving all my power to God then sitting and waiting. I, too, needed to be working at answering my own prayers by setting goals and taking actions. I also learned that having faith is accepting my inner voice's wisdom when exercising my will by making choices. I can attest that having faith in oneself and—as in my case—God truly helps to build self-trust.

Rewards of Faith in Prayer

It is clear now why many times it appeared that my prayers went unanswered when I did not get my expected outcomes. In those situations, what I did not realize was that God had better plans for me than what I could have conjured up by my limited desires. This should never have surprised me because I always ended my prayer requests with, "...Please answer my prayer if it is your plan for me, and is in the best interest of all involved."

My prayers have evolved to where I do not ask for specific outcomes, but instead, I pray that I may receive the courage to face the challenge and to change in me what I must, the strength to accept what I cannot change, the insight to help me understand the person or situation, the help to forgive when needed, patience with everything and everyone, and the faith to carry on. I also ask that I be shown clearly what I must do. Again, these prayers are with complete faith that God hears me and is looking after me.

When I asked God to show me how to live my life purpose, I never would have imagined the answer would be through hemiplegia and then hemiparesis. I now understand I was given nothing more than I could handle. In order to serve God, I needed to experience loss at a profound level. The stroke losses spiraled me into the depths of my soul. As I learned to accept and work with the losses, no amount of darkness could suppress my growing inner strength. This inner strength eventually anchored in me the desire to maintain a healthy state of mind and forged the character to weather all storms of life.

I was disappointed in not getting a resource teaching position for the fall of 2004. I had thought that would be the best thing for me. I could not understand why God would not grant me this.

I now know I had lessons to learn. I needed to learn about letting go and not controlling my destiny, but to trust in God. Having the stroke at the end of September gave me the advantage of staying at my school where I knew everyone and would have their needed support after my stroke. Staying in a classroom teaching role, in which I had taught half the students when they were in grade three, guaranteed that I had an established bond with those students, and could focus on creating new bonds with the other students in our short three weeks together. These bonds with students and the support of staff provided a lot of love and care at a critical time. I believe that God had a hand in keeping me in the same school to guarantee the support of my students and their families.

Faith in the Darkest Hours

Faith is believing when it is beyond the power of reason to believe.—Voltaire

I tried to hang on to what little faith I had like a terrified child clinging to a parent. Any courage to face the damages of stroke escaped me. I was a coward. In those moments, I found it difficult to believe that God had not abandoned me, and to trust that he would provide what I needed. All this was too much to digest. Eventually, the fear extinguished hope. The expectations for a functional, normal life waned because of my losses. In panic, I invoked the help of God, Jesus, the angels and any divine beings out there, because I knew that I could not overcome the shock of all my losses by myself. Heck, I even asked for faith, self-trust, courage, inner strength, and the ability to attune my ears to my inner voice.

The shock of discovering that my whole left side could no longer move as I willed it was frightening—overwhelming! Incomprehensible! Being preoccupied with fear added another fear that I might become deaf to divine inner wisdom. For that reason, I asked God to attune my senses so I would not miss any signs of his presence and his guidance through my inner voice.

In the past, my strength of character and faith had often helped me survive many adversities. So why not now? God had always been with me so He must still be here. I desperately wanted help to get me through this experience. I knew I needed more than therapy, family, and friends. It was then that my daily prayers often became hourly, sometimes minutes apart.

I longed for distraction from the painful reality of my paralysis and its enveloping darkness of challenges. It was difficult to live joyfully, to see brightness in anything, so I added to my prayers the request for some kind of relief. This relief came in bouts of spontaneous, inappropriate laughter—medically called *emotional incontinence* or *emotional lability*.

I was relieved to learn that my emotional shortcomings had a legitimate explanation. My acquired brain damage caused emotional outbursts, often with uncontrollable laughter framed in an exaggerated smile. This occurred when I felt sadness, concern, or upset, from seeing someone hurt or when I was feeling hurt. People who did not know this about me might have thought I was rude, inappropriate or even insensitive. Even though I was very much aware it was not a laughter of joy, I would be confused about my inappropriate laughter and equally embarrassed.

The many times I laughed inappropriately and which caused me embarrassment, I never looked at that as a curse, but instead, as an opportunity to educate others about emotional incontinence. When I explained this condition to others, they usually laughed with me. The relief of laughter was a delightful answer to my prayer for joy.

Many times, to re-energize my faith in God, I would think about what my mémère Emond taught me about faith and prayer. The most momentous and meaningful lesson learned was when I was a preschooler. One day, mémère Emond taught me how to pray to God and to St. Antoine (St. Anthony), the patron saint of lost causes, things, or items. When my younger brother was a toddler, he had accidentally dropped my mother's wedding ring from a kitchen cupboard shelf and it was lost. As he and my mother frantically searched for her ring, mémère Emond took my hand and insisted I follow her to her room even though my mom clearly needed my help. She had me sit in front of Jesus' picture on her wall and said he would help me find the ring. She adamantly explained that one tiny droplet of doubt while praying would be enough to sabotage any prayer. Like any eager apprentice, I listened attentively to her every word on how to pray, and repeated her guiding words as she led us in prayer to Jesus and St. Antoine. I recall concentrating intently on every word and only allowing myself to believe that Jesus, St. Antoine, and God heard every word. Once we were finished praying, we walked back into the living room. As I stepped on its threshold, I looked down on the carpet and to my delight and awe I spotted my mom's ring on the carpet. Mémère Emond looked at me and her eyes expressed proudly, "I told you your prayer would be answered!" That became my first of many answered prayers to God and his saints. Since then, I've learned that God has an army of helpers like his angels and more are available to support and assist me in my prayer requests.

This valuable lesson about prayer reminded me how doubt had often been a barrier between me and my soul or God. Throughout the painful stroke experiences, and other challenges, I have had my share of doubts. Still to this day, whenever I feel alone and hurt I remind myself that God is with me, and that his love is present through loving words, the cardinal who visits me regularly, or by random acts of kindness from a family member or friend. I choose to see his presence in all these gestures.

There Are Valuable Life Lessons in all Adversities

Of all the major life changing challenges I experienced, my stroke recovery was the one that taught me the most-valuable life lessons. Many people express that they don't know how I survived the ordeal. Well, truth be told, there were several major events of crisis in my life that I have had to overcome. I've chosen not to discuss them in this book to protect and respect the privacy of other people.

In the beginning of intense stroke recovery, I had to focus solely on my physical body and rely on the strength of my soul to survive. Then, when the time was right I engaged my other three bodies. Although I could not physically dance for many years post stroke, I did learn the more-important Dance of Life. That is, the dance of engaging all my bodies in daily living. My physical body, mind body, spiritual body, and psychological body each had an important role in the dance.

Learning: How I Turned My Negative Emotions Around

Since my stroke, I've come to understand how anger, resentment, and bitterness, as well as the use of negative or hurtful words, have a life of their own. They vibrate in waves that attract destructive, lower energies and reactions from other people. These energies do not nurture optimal emotional and spiritual well-being for anyone.

How did I raise my negative energy level to a productive, peaceful and positive level when I had so much anger after the stroke? To begin with, I wasn't enjoying the negative emotions inside me and I certainly didn't want others to find out I had them. Therefore, I needed to create positive ones around me. In a nutshell, I did the following.

GRATITUDE

I thanked God every day for being alive even though I did not know why I was saying this. You ask why one might thank God for hemiplegia? Whenever I asked myself that question, I would remind myself that I was still alive, I had a dedicated husband, a supportive and loving family, friends, and a second chance to fulfill my life purpose. I kept thanking God, and eventually I felt *genuine* gratitude and appreciation for still being alive. As a result, my attitude changed accordingly. It became easy to believe I had been blessed rather than punished.

POSITIVE WORDS AND THOUGHTS

I focused on a positive attitude that helped generate thoughts, words, then emotions of love, joy, compassion, and loving, kind gestures. Positive energy generated by positive thoughts and words fueled me toward thinking and acting positively

VISUALIZATION

Visualizing what I want my body to do was a strategy I practiced throughout my recovery and still do today. For example, for many years, I watched cooking shows on the food channel. I pretended my hands were the chef's hands preparing the food, especially the left hand. I imagined how the food felt in my hands: smooth, wet and cool. I studied how the fingers grasped and manipulated the food, and how the utensils were handled. I stared at how the fingers skillfully cut, chopped, and stirred the food. I pretended it was my hand making the chopping noise and echoing the metal sound of whisked ingredients throughout the kitchen. I imagined smelling the ingredients as they squirted the aromas into my nostrils, and my mouth salivating into my taste buds. I visualized my face happy to be actively cooking again and my body feeling the joy in plating the food for family and friends. All the while, I believed I would some day do this again. Today, I can use my left hand in food preparation and although it is more of a helping hand than a chef's skillful hand, I am productive in the kitchen again, which brings me great satisfaction.

RANDOM ACTS OF KINDNESS

I also seized every opportunity in which I could perform kind gestures for others. Yes, this was possible even when I was in a wheelchair and still in hospital. In my small ways, I would seek opportunities to lend a helping hand to fellow patients. This in turn eventually gave me feelings of peace and joy, and increased my self-worth—and my compassion for others.

ENTRUST NEGATIVE THOUGHTS TO GOD

When negative thoughts appeared, I acknowledged that I had them and told myself that God had beautiful plans in store for me so I offered any unwanted thoughts to God. I needed to trust that I would experience God's beautiful plans for me in due time, and so I did.

Shortly after the strokes, the doctors were reluctant to give a definite prognosis of recovery. In an effort to not be discouraged by what this possibly meant, I decided to view myself as an artist, an artist whose future was a blank canvas on which I was free to paint anything I wanted, and to use any color. I creatively painted a picture of a life of hope by using vibrant colors that symbolized positive emotions. To keep focused on this visualization, I relied on the positive and loving emotional help of my husband, family and dear friends. This allowed the artist in me, inspired by a friend's painting, to paint a landscape with bold, strong mountains draped in nourishing and energizing waterfalls flowing into lakes. The peaceful shining lakes reflected glimmering starlit or sunlit diamonds on their surfaces. I would see myself walking as normally as possible without a cane along the water's edge in a lush, green valley. This vision included the hope that I would someday be able to move my arm, hand and fingers. If I achieved more than a minimal functional level, I would see it as an added blessing.

The Healing Power of Smiling and Loving Kindness

While in the physical rehab hospital, I asked myself how I overcame previous challenges. I thought of how I rose above some traumatic, painful, and emotionally scarring events in my lifetime. Then, I thought of an incident that taught me the importance of never underestimating the healing power of a smile and expressing loving kindness toward others. It was a time during my adolescence when I was feeling much sadness and how often life had not seemed worthy of smiling.

I was 14 years old and waitressing in an ice cream parlor/restaurant. It was a sunny Sunday morning and I was alone opening and setting up the restaurant. Every time I passed by the tables along the front expanse of east-facing windows, the sun radiated golden bright, penetrating rays and, when in its path, I felt its soothing warmth on my body. Despite my sadness, I somehow always could read and appreciate moments like these as loving gestures from God.

Today, moments like these continue to make me always feel nature is God's wonderful way of giving grace.

That morning, business in the restaurant was peculiarly quiet. My first customer, a young man, sat on a stool, at a service counter, with his back to the windows. After I served him his breakfast, a woman, probably not more than forty-five, entered the premises. She sat at a table against the window behind the young man. I could see the sun bathed her too, in the comfort of its warmth.

I couldn't help but notice her tired eyes were as despondent as her demeanor. As we discussed the breakfast menu, I sensed her struggles were unbearable. I then not only saw intense melancholy in her eyes but my heart suddenly filled with compassion for hers. I never got her name and for the sake of this story, I shall name her Sunny Day Lady because of how our brief encounter profoundly influenced my life. Our encounter taught me to believe that God sends us people to inform us, guide us, and to teach each other lessons.

Kindness is more than deeds. It is an attitude, an expression, a look, a touch. It is anything that lifts another person.—Anonymous

One of the many qualities I earned from surviving a childhood with a chronic, alcoholic father is developing a keen awareness of sensing strong emotions in others. That day, a strong urge overcame me to greet Sunny Day Lady with a smile and be extra attentive. It just seemed like the right thing to do. At that time, I probably felt this intense reaction because her sadness touched my own. Even then, it was a subconscious pattern of mine to cover up my sadness with smiles and to give a lot of attention to people, because deep inside, I hoped they would reciprocate. However, on that day, this was not the case. I strongly sensed the importance to simply be a humble giver of genuine, loving kindness.

When life gives you a hundred reasons to cry, show life that you have a thousand reasons to smile.—Anonymous

I was attentive to her needs without being intrusive and always while smiling warmly. When Sunny Day Lady paid for the bill, she requested a few moments of my time. I politely and curiously accepted. She explained she had spent all night walking and had decided to commit suicide that morning. However, something inside her urged her to first come into the restaurant. Sunny Day Lady didn't know why she was there, but when I greeted her with a smile she said she wanted to stay and eat. Tearfully she thanked me for changing her mind about committing suicide because I was someone who cared and valued her. Our encounter had renewed her hope and courage to continue living. This powerful and emotional encounter left me speechless.

Young and inexperienced, I was also uncertain as to how I could respond accordingly and with words of encouragement. I could only utter—yes, with a smile—"You are welcome. Thank you. God bless you."

She thanked me once again for giving her a reason to live and left as quickly as she had entered my life. I never saw her again.

When I turned around, I saw the young man at the counter crying. His tears confirmed the significance of that moment. I could allow myself to acknowledge my own overwhelming emotions in the back kitchen. I did not tell anyone about this for many years because I did not want anyone's opinions to tarnish my sacred experience. Now, no one can because I know God sends us each other as angels of hope, courage, and blessings.

Sunny Day Lady had the courage to verbalize what many people would never admit. She could have left the restaurant without telling me anything. I believe this was a divine intervention, and not only for Sunny Day Lady, but also for me many decades later during my stroke recovery when I needed it most. God's omnipresent grace in our lives amazes me how far-reaching and long lasting it is. This profound experience with Sunny Day Lady had taught me never to underestimate the healing power of a smile.

Weeks after September 29, 2004, I remembered my encounter with Sunny Day Lady and was inspired to believe that I could still have a meaningful life, and that I could come to value it regardless of my physical circumstances. Once again, I was motivated to smile but this time for me. I too, had experienced a valuable epiphany on that fine Sunday morning: smiling renews hope, courage and strength for a better life. If my smile could save a stranger's life then I needed to believe it could save mine!

Smiling for any reason, even if only for small moments, re-introduced joy into my life, especially at a time when I had imagined this was unlikely. I no longer took for granted insignificant events. As the small joys became easier to smile at, it became easier to continue smiling, even as a hemiplegic—or now as a hemiparetic.

Never frown because you never know who might be falling in love with your smile.—Justine Milton

I have come to believe that the divine encounter with Sunny Day Lady has served me many times throughout my life. God loves us so much he wants us to know we're not alone. My smile and kindness inspired in Sunny Day Lady the will to continue living, and she gave *me* the insight to see that *my* life had meaning even at 14 years of age. And now, again at 42. I learned a lesson about the alternative to suicide. Unexpected new and renewed joys can be a delightful end to painful experiences or give a reprieve from painful life conditions. Therefore, when I became hemiplegic, smiling kept me far away from wanting to die. Smiling inspired me to live with courage and with the belief that I would find more joys and peace.

Smiling and Eye Contact

Sunny Day Lady also inspired me to face my biggest fear on my first outing from the rehab hospital. The world outside the hospital terrified me because I hadn't experienced it from a wheelchair. That was more frightening than being in the wheelchair. I didn't think anyone I was with would understand this so I hid my fears behind my smiles. The bigger the smile, the bigger the fear I covered.

As I ventured into my first public wheelchair outing to Sunday Mass at church, I was fearful and awkward, nervous. It seemed bizarre and unnatural to enter the church in a wheelchair I didn't understand why I felt self-conscious and embarrassed. These emotions intensified when I sensed many pairs of eyes watching me. Suddenly, a clear and calm inner voice said "Smile." Knowing that this was the easiest thing for me to do since my stroke and how it always made me feel better, I forced a big smile.

That day in church, everyone greeted me with returned smiles instead of with looks of pity. I believe it's in large part because I smiled first at them so appeared to be happy. Smiling is an excellent armor. Their caring reception raised my spirits and reinforced that smiling does positively influence one's world. Later, I realized, from my church visit, that I did not fear people's judgment of my physical disabilities so much as that their pity might weaken me emotionally.

From that point on, I chose to sport a smile in public, regardless of a wheelchair, strangers' stares, a cane, an unsightly foot orthotic, my unsteady gait, or whatever mood I was in. Subsequently, smiling became a way to maintain a positive attitude in the face of difficult situations. Still today, because of my emotional incontinence, I express sudden discomfort, surprise, and even malaise with a smile. As the years progress, my emotional incontinence happens less because my smiles remain my armor.

I also learned that day in church that smiling wasn't enough to protect me from fear. I needed to look fear in the eye which meant, as I smiled, I needed to look people in the eye. They needed to see that I had hope in mine and I needed to see hope or joy in theirs. Being determined to smile—coupled with making eye contact—provided me with generous opportunities to feel connected to an unfamiliar world. With those connections, I experienced acceptance, comfort, safety, and nurturing.

----- Original Message -----
From: Louis Barre
Sent: Monday, October 25, 2004 1:27 AM
Subject: Carole Update – Day 27

On Saturday, we left "Club Rehab" for the first over-nighter at Carole's parents. The soft, and big, bed was a very nice treat. Sunday morning, we went to church as per our usual routine, enjoyed a bad cup of coffee with a few good friends in the basement afterwards, and had a great brunch with dear friends. Life seemed somewhat normal! Everyone who sees Carole welcomes her with kindness and enthusiasm. It is this positive energy that helps so much to keep her motivated.

Thank you.
Louis

Daily Gratitude

Years after my stroke, an inspirational teacher explained to me that in the face of challenge, always give thanks to God because this simple act of gratitude offers us grace and God's mercy. Those words reminded me of how I gave thanks for still being alive despite my hemiplegia. In the early hospital days, I oddly thanked God and Jesus numerous times a day without knowing why I was so thankful. I somehow knew deep in my soul that blessings would come out of expressing simple gratitude. Sure enough, it became easier to find things or gestures for which to be thankful. The caring nurse, the stranger's smile, a caring friend, a loving family, and the ongoing support I received. The grace I had to see all the kind gestures of love and support gave me inner strength and insight to guide me along the journey. It was a choice to be receptive, to accept, and be thankful.

Since re-igniting my awareness of how smiling helps ensure I have more life-giving interactions, I noted something about my exchange of smiles and eye contacts with some strangers. When some passersby saw me smiling warmly at them as I established eye contact, they would respond respectively. Brief as these encounters were, it seemed as though more happened than glances. People who seemed sad gave a second look at my smile and would then not resist looking me in the eyes while smiling back, looking somewhat cheerfully boosted. I couldn't help but feel in those moments, gratitude for those intimate blessings.

These observations were evidence enough to convince me how important it was to smile, to have direct eye contact with acquaintances, our dear ones, and strangers. It is a way of sending warm greetings out into our world, which, I believe, is in dire need of it.

The word Namaste, which means "I bow to the divinity within you," salutes that divinity whenever we make eye contact with each other. Thoughtful eye contact is a caring gesture that honors the divine soul in another human being. When I smile at panhandlers and street people, they often look to be in disbelief that I have acknowledged their presence. I never feel threatened because at some deep level I know our souls have connected and there is an unspoken respect. Through the encounters of respectful and peaceful eye contact, I have experienced safety, warmth, joy, and even peace. I no longer try to avoid eye contact. When I take the time to have eye contact and genuinely smile, I believe it is to the soul of the person before me. At some level, I believe this has an impact on someone's life and on mine. For that I am grateful because I know at some subconscious level, it works.

Feeling gratitude for everyday little things gave me genuine happiness and made me feel alive even though I was half-paralyzed for a long time.

A friend once asked me, years after I could freely walk again, if I had the choice, would I do it all over again. "Without a doubt," I answered peacefully. "Yes. I would choose to survive my paralyzing stroke."

He appeared shocked by my answer.

Even though I felt he didn't understand where I was coming from, it was clear to me why I had answered so confidently and without hesitation. It was worth all that I had learned about how to live my life by leaving it in God's hands, the gems of insights, and the countless more blessings I received. I know that in order to come to these realizations, I needed to walk alone in the deepest darkness—my darkness was hemiplegia. I received what I needed to survive this adversity because I allowed my heart to be receptive and that lesson in itself brought much joy.

For today and its blessings, I owe the world an attitude of gratitude.—Anonymous

Gratitude was significant to my recovery and it continues to be powerful in my life. It also opened my mind to understanding how the word gratitude itself is meaningful. I see two words in the word gratitude: grace and attitude. The root word in gratitude is attitude minus a "t" and the prefix "gra" is in the word grace minus the "ce." Both of these words are important when expressing gratitude because with the attitude of thankfulness, gifts of grace are given. When I expressed daily gratitude to God because I was still alive, I received grace through all his messengers of family, friends and strangers when I least expected it. This grace appeared in GEMS of laughter, love, and words of hope. Today, gratitude still rewards me with precious GEMS.

Laughter and gratitude helped me cope with hemiplegia and slowly dissolved bitterness, self-pity, resentment, and anger. The simple daily exercise of gratitude opened my eyes to see—each day—all the wonderful blessings and the goodness in others. There was the caring, attentive ward assistant who regularly took the time to talk to me and value me as a human being. She knew it was important that I have a daily shower, and despite the rules, she ensured there was an available shower stall for me. Liette, a close friend, gave of her limited time to clean my house once a week for several months after the hospital discharge. The list goes on. Finding many reasons for daily gratitude became easier as I received increased self-awareness, faith, joy and laughter, all nurturing a positive attitude.

Laughter amid Adversity

Laughter in the midst of adversity is a good thing, not a crazy thing. Many times during my recovery and other life challenges, I welcomed laughter as a form of relief. It helped soothe sadness or anxiety.

Smiling releases happy hormones that make us feel better. Research proves laughter releases endorphins that decrease the levels of stress hormones of cortisol and adrenaline. Research also proves that laughter can have a positive effect on our mood and allows our immune system to work more effectively. So, then, why not laugh?

To be half-paralyzed naturally presented serious moments and situations of awkwardness that would make people feel uncomfortable or saddened. Therefore, every chance I had, I turned around these awkward moments of mobility that could be seen as slapstick comedy into buckets of laughter. For example, on my first day pass from the rehab hospital, I spent the day at my mother's house. She gave me a fortune cookie and when it was my turn to read it aloud my sister, my mother, and I looked at each other and burst out into laughter. It read, "You will dance to a different beat next summer." To cry "woe is me" at that moment would have made us all feel despair about my losses. Instead, laughter lightened up the situation. How serendipitous that I had taped the fortune message to the inside cover of the book in my hand: *Laughing out Loud: A Collection of Heavenly Humor* by Martha Bolton.

Since my stroke, laughter has invited me to live with good feelings and a positive attitude. Not just any kind of laughter brings joy. Laughter at the expense of someone else or teasing laughter is not helpful, but hurtful. It is not a pick-me-up but a destructive putdown—although every time I chose to laugh about my physical awkwardness post stroke, or during other life circumstances, it was about the humor in the situation and not about me.

At Club Rehab, laughter and smiling became my preferred coping mechanisms. When I felt embarrassed, angry, sad, or frustrated by clumsy attempts to move my limp, left side, I made jokes as an invitation for others to laugh with me. I noticed that my laughter was infectious and affected the attitudes of my caregivers. It was easier for them to be with me.

Sadly, I could not sustain this after the hospital discharge because of stroke-induced depression. It took seven years of prescribed antidepressants, meditation practices, and CBT (cognitive behavior therapy) to help restore this chemical imbalance. However, because of the brain damage, I still need to practice CBT continuously, and meditate regularly to compensate for the lingering cognitive brain damage.

I still choose to laugh, when it fits, to make difficult situations easier to face and digest. This influences the energy around me to be light, positive, and pleasant. Plenty of reason to laugh and continue smiling!

Attitude and the Power of Positive Thinking

There is little difference in people, but that little difference makes a big difference. The little difference is attitude. The big difference is whether it is positive or negative. —Clement Stone

In the days following my stroke, the medications' curtain of heavy drowsiness slowly wore off enough to show me my physical losses. In disbelief of what had happened to me and thinking it was all a big mistake, I was flooded with anxious, dark, fearful thoughts. Then my emotions invited me to the brink of seeking justice and this mission evoked a negative attitude. However, by the grace of God, I had enough insight to know that if I allowed myself to stay with these dark thoughts, I'd drown in the ocean of self-pity. This insight also helped me see that my children were my motivation to be an inspiration.

I couldn't let myself worry about them because that too would depress me. In my eyes, and possibly in those of my children, it would have been cowardly of me to give up and be miserable. I had to focus on being determined, strong and brave—not weak and defeated. After all, I had always prided myself in rising above any crisis. It then became very clear that I wanted to survive this for my children. I would be the phoenix rising from her ashes.

I discovered I always have choices and sometimes it is only a choice of attitude.—Anonymous

Finding courage and strength to have a positive attitude and mindset became my mission. I began to rely on the love and support of family and friends, and in believing there was healing power in smiling, daily gratitude, laughter, and everyone's prayers for us. Insignificant as these might seem, I soon learned how they are certainly powerfully effective. A positive attitude gave me the strength to overcome from the smallest to the biggest hurdles in stroke recovery.

Attracting Positive Energy in Our Lives
We never know how far reaching something
We may think, say or do today
Will affect the lives of millions tomorrow.
—BJ Palmer

While in the hospital, when people greeted me with a genuine smile, positive comments or a happy disposition, this helped me forget I was confined to a wheelchair. These positive interactions inspired me to further experiment not only with smiles, but also with how my thoughts, words and actions influenced my world and the worlds of others. When I deliberately smiled at everyone, including strangers, I also spoke and behaved with the attitude and belief that my glass was half full. I somehow knew this would prove to me that I had the power to create a positive, nurturing environment. Despite the uncertainty of my physical recovery, this was a way to get reassurance in knowing that I had control somewhere in my life.

Attitudes are contagious. Is yours worth catching?—Anonymous

As I experienced more joy and satisfaction in my interactions with others, I learned how it was not up to those around me to create the joy I wanted, but for me to create it for myself. The role I played in my interactions with others sent a subtle message that I wanted joy and hope in my life. I hadn't realized my attitude was like sending a magnetic signal out into the world to attract what I needed to achieve my desires. The law of attraction!

Hospital staff, family and friends soon viewed me as an upbeat, positive patient. Family and friends often commented on how they admired my strength. In fact, I had very little strength. I mainly relied on receiving it from others' positive, life-giving energy exchanged between us. Smiling was my tool to acquire this. It was far more beneficial to all that I saw myself as a source of positive energy going out into the world than to be responsible for negative outcomes. After all, to walk and to move my left hand and arm again was my responsibility. I needed to achieve this with courage, patience, strength, and hope, and it was up to me to cultivate and attract it.

This valuable lesson of knowing that I am in control of how the world interacts with me is one I still live by today. Human as I am, I do, however, stumble from to time but I always manage to find my way back to these truths. In those situations, the negative energy I create circles right back to me. It has what I call a boomerang effect on me and on those from whom I need emotional support and life-giving relationships. Whenever this occurs, the boomerang effect always prompts me to assess and redirect my thoughts and attitudes in a positive direction. The new lesson in this is to forgive myself and move healthily forward when I fall into old negative thinking patterns.

It is a conscious decision to nurture a positive attitude. Adopting the view early on that my stroke was an opportunity instead of a curse was a step toward keeping a positive attitude and frame of mind. It became easier to maintain the mindset that my life is filled with opportunities for growth and to find new meanings in my life.

I'm not saying that I never feel tempted into negative thinking. I'm saying that when this occurs, I persist at finding reasons to view my glass as half full, much like appreciating a precious rose without letting the thorny stem ruin its beauty. Despite painful experiences, I know I can become a better person for others and for myself and that these experiences won't kill me.

Staying on the high road means searching for light amid dark situations no matter how small the twinkle of a "gem." I choose to accept this tiny twinkle as a shimmer of hope. I do not allow myself to look back at what was; this would have been too painful. I face reality and look ahead at what could possibly be regardless of how much this might require me to be demanding and courageous. It is a practice of blind faith and trust in God.

Maintaining Healthy Thoughts and Feelings

A little over a year and a half after the stroke, I participated in a free physiotherapy program offered by a medical department from a local university. Before I attended this program, I had learned through personal research that effective stroke recovery is more likely with an immediate, consistent and ongoing intensive therapy program. I shared this newfound knowledge with a therapist in the program whose comments I did not expect. He told me if I wanted such a program, I should have paid for it in the United States and further stated there are many excellent, private programs that could have better addressed my stroke recovery needs. That response angered me because like so many other stroke survivors, I could not afford this and didn't think I should have to go to another country to get the medical help I need.

For over a week I obsessed about his unexpected response. This obsession then morphed into anger until I gained insight about its true nature. I was not angry at the therapist's response but rather about the window of opportunity I had missed for the best recovery by not having received immediate and aggressive therapy. Then my anger shifted to the provincial medical system that had not provided an effective therapy program for stroke survivors like me. But then I had to realize that in spite of these public health program shortfalls, I was blessed to have received what I did: in many countries there are no public health programs.

This bout of negative emotion made me wonder if stopping antidepressants three weeks earlier had been responsible. Eight months later, when my employer's disability case manager and vocational therapist observed that this indeed was happening they referred me to a neuropsychologist. Fortunately, I had an employee disability plan to fund the services of a psychologist. I needed to address my increasing grief and the mental processing difficulties I was experiencing with increasing anxiety.

This is when I learned that the stroke had affected my ability to process emotions. The neuropsychologist explained the benefits of antidepressants and CBT in managing these deficits. For stroke patients with brain damage predisposing us to depression, this therapy model in conjunction with antidepressants, I was told, would be helpful. This convinced me it was worth a try. Incidentally, from what I've learned, CBT can benefit everyone.

When I learned how to use basic CBT practices in my life, I also learned the following: Our thoughts are the cause for our feelings and behaviors, not external things like people, situations, and events. Cognitive behavior therapy is a model based on this. The intent of this model is to become aware of our thoughts and patterns in order to help improve the way we think, so that we have better control of our feelings and actions. [David D. Burns, 1999]

I had sustained brain damage to the region of my brain that affects serotonin re-uptake levels. It uses up too much serotonin, therefore, I needed antidepressants to stabilize my serotonin levels. In other words, it is much like a car needing repairs to ensure it does not burn too much oil and to maintain a sufficient oil level in the engine for smooth operation. Gaining this new knowledge alleviated my concerns about losing control of my mind and made it easier to accept that I had to continue taking antidepressants.

Eighteen months after the stroke, I stopped taking antidepressants because my psychologist and I felt I might be ready. My brain felt different. I knew who I had been was fundamentally changed even though to others I did not appear to be, nor seem to communicate any differently than I did, pre-stroke.

The misfiring of my brain's neurons still occurs today. More often than not my brain is slow to recognize that I have an emotional reaction to something or someone, and if something is too upsetting, my brain files the event away until I can process it. The antidepressants softened, or as in my case, completely numbed, any emotional response while I took them up until the autumn of 2011.

A hidden domino effect happens in my processing of information when an event or comment stirs much-needed responses. Immediately, I'm like a deer in the headlights. I become numb, non-reactive, while my brain shifts into slow gear. It's as though I am on hold, waiting for my brain synapses to signal how to think and feel. I guess my silence to others sends the wrong message because they often drop or change the subject when they get no response from me. Consequently, their reactions distract me from waiting for mine and I forget what has just happened. Often, it takes a while before it is clear to me why I respond a certain way or why I am upset. My response gets shelved somewhere until, sometimes, up to months later when something will trigger it, and suddenly I'm flooded with thoughts and emotions that I don't understand.

As soon as these emotions emerge—if I'm in a calm environment —I can remember to practice CBT, correct any misguiding thoughts, and act appropriately. As I gain more experience and awareness in remembering to stop and think, I am less impulsive in my reactions, which happens to be another stroke-acquired behavior I'm learning to deal with. However, if I'm in a situation already emotional or upsetting, I might react impulsively and even emotionally irrationally. This is difficult for my family because it requires patience from of all of us to understand my emotional reactions or lack thereof when there ought to be some. Therefore, I must work harder than most people to be aware of my thoughts and how they affect my feelings.

Today, I know I must follow a regular routine in meditating, practicing CBT, and performing physical exercise. When I do this, I can then come from a calm state of mind in those awkward situations where clarity of thought and emotion is beneficial, not to mention being attuned to my inner voice. The most important of the three must-dos is meditating. There are many studies done using EEGs that demonstrated increased brain waves through meditation and which lead to an increase of a relaxed state, relaxed alertness, creative thinking and focused, calm thinking. The less I meditate, the less I am in control of my cognitive deficits and emotions.

Maintaining a Positive Attitude

Whenever I slip into a negative attitude, I observe people's reactions becoming less positive and uncomfortable. In these situations, the negative energy I have created circles right back to me. It has that boomerang effect on me and on those from whom I need emotional support. When this occurs, it reminds me to direct my attitude in a positive direction.

A great attitude does much more than turn on the lights in our worlds; it seems to magically connect us to all sorts of serendipitous opportunities that were somehow absent before the change.
—Anonymous

It is a conscious decision to nurture a positive attitude. Thinking back to when I adopted the view that my stroke was an opportunity instead of a curse, was a step in the direction toward always keeping that positive frame of mind. This attitude helped to maintain a vision of opportunities for growth and to find new meanings about my life. That is not to say that after my stroke, I never felt cursed or negative about my situation. I continued to seek reasons to view my glass as half full. Much like a rose is still beautiful in spite of its thorny stem, my stroke contained beauty in spite of the losses that came with it. Regardless of my painful experience, I believed I would become a better person for others and myself.

I stay on the high road by searching for the bright side of dark situations. I avoid looking back at what was; this can be painful. I face reality and look ahead at what can be no matter how demanding of courage this requires of me.

If you look at only what is, you might never attain what could be.
—Anonymous

Reflecting on these previous experiences reminds me of what I learned from them and how I must continue to apply this knowledge in all life challenges and events. Recounting these stories proves that God blessed me with these life lessons for more than pragmatic reasons: they equipped me for stroke survival. The lesson such as the Sunny Day Lady some twenty-eight years earlier, later manifested into new mini-miracles by bringing about new blessings of insight and inspiration.

Today, despite how much is on my plate, I continue to believe that God is present in my continuous recovery and life. Knowing this helps me to eat my challenges with gratitude and grace instead of spitting them out and starving from despair, doubt and lost purpose. The by-products of choosing the high road are hope, faith, courage, peace, and self-trust.

A rose only becomes beautiful and blesses others when it opens up and blooms. Its greatest tragedy is to stay in a tight-closed bud, never fulfilling its potential.—Anonymous

Receptivity of Mind and Soul to Attract Positive Outcomes

Never had I understood as well as I do now about how my thoughts truly influence what happens around me. When I have a receptive mind for all that is good in people, situations, and expectations, I attract positive outcomes. However stressful, life challenges can sometimes complicate this. For example, had I agreed with people who judged someone close to me was unredeemable because of a drastic, poor choice he had made, we would have abandoned him, failed him. This would have devastated his life and that of those close to him—I would never have been able to forgive myself. Thankfully, he did turn his life around and I suspect my decision to support this person was and still is significant.

When I find myself in situations where conversations are negative, I try to influence them in a positive direction so we will all leave feeling hope, acceptance, tolerance, kindness, or joy appropriate to the situation. I prefer to surround myself with like-minded people because life is much more pleasant that way, and we all leave each other feeling energized. But this doesn't mean I wear rose-colored glasses.

I always worried about what others thought of me or my family during life challenges before the stroke. Precious energies were spent on fretting, and through excessive thought patterns that usually ended up as negative, tangled ideas. None of it ever gave me peace of mind. Hemiplegia forced me to learn the benefits of making rational interpretations of others' words and actions and setting realistic expectations of others. This avoided disappointment and hurt feelings.

To Give or Not to Give
Power to Others' Actions

Each morning when I open my eyes I say to myself: I, not events, have the power to make me happy or unhappy today. I can choose which it shall be. Yesterday is dead, tomorrow hasn't arrived yet. I have just one day, today, and I'm going to be happy in it.
—Groucho Marx

Even though the next stories I share don't relate to others' reactions, they describe how I didn't let my reaction to my changed appearance affect how I felt about myself.

It wasn't clear to me how much physical loss I had sustained from the stroke until I got up to go to the washroom for the first time in the hospital. It took Louis and a nurse to maneuver me from my bed to the toilet. Once there, I looked up into the mirror and was horrified by my half-drooping face. I was shocked to see a face that was supposed to be mine but I was too weak physically and psychologically to react, or care, that the person staring back at me didn't look like me. I saw a stranger. I could only conjure the idea that my body was on hiatus somewhere and hope it would come back to find me. I didn't have the wherewithal to let myself fear that it would not. All I could think was that it must. It must!

The second story is of my first encounter with someone's reactions to my changed body. In the first weeks after the stroke, I was often transported by wheelchair to appointments throughout the hospital. When I saw my reflections in mirrors or glass panes, I did not recognize me. Who was this person slouched to the left with a dazed look and her mouth hanging open? I wanted a poster to announce to the world, "This really is NOT me! I just don't have the strength to keep my mouth closed." I thought I looked like a person typically portrayed in movies with mental and physical disabilities. Although I was not, the passersby did not know this, and that bothered me! It saddened me that I was too physically broken to do anything about this.

The person underneath this pitiful exterior was indeed alive, creative, intelligent, and passionate. We all have a purpose for being here and deserve recognition and respect. I wanted so much for everyone to know or think of this as they stared at me or pretended not to see me.

Some people looked at me—or *through* me. Some even expressed visible disgust or fear or both. These reactions left me feeling undignified, insignificant. For the first time, I experienced what it feels like for people living in physically challenged bodies with healthy minds. To be treated as unworthy of regard or notice made me feel vulnerable and demeaned.

The third event I'd like to share epitomizes how a person didn't consider my feelings. An orderly was transporting me in my wheelchair for tests in the hospital. I recognized someone from our church, sitting at a table in a hallway cafe. Although we had never spoken to each other at church, we often smiled, said hello or nodded to each other. I smiled at her. She looked at me twice, and as I smiled at her again, I waved with my right hand. I couldn't see her response because by then she was far behind me. When I passed there again after my appointment, she was still sitting there and looked at me. She turned her head away quickly but not quickly enough to hide her disgusted expression. I interpreted this at the time that she was embarrassed by my attempt to interact with her.

Had she not recognized me? Had she thought I was a stranger? Had she been taken aback by a stranger's reaching out to her? Had my appearance disgusted her? Or had all this made *her* feel uncomfortable? I will never know. Even though, it took all my internal strength not to cry on the spot. I felt rejected and hurt. Devastated. Obviously, I was not the healthy woman she saw in church on Sundays, but was I that unrecognizable?

What did I want from her? I certainly did not want her to look at me with disgust. Just a simple nod, maybe even a smile acknowledging my presence would have been kind. Something I am certain I probably would have received before my stroke.

I decided to give her the benefit of the doubt and forgive her. Was she aware of her reaction and its impact on me? I will never know. I guess most of us are never fully aware of how our actions affect others. I also couldn't help but question if I, too, had ever reacted similarly to someone in a wheelchair or with a notable disability. If so, that would be awful. Feeling guilt of this kind, or any other, is unproductive. Therefore, I am choosing to forgive myself for any such thing I might have done to another person.

The grace that came from this forgiveness was that I was able to interact kindly with this woman without any negative emotions in subsequent church encounters. It was easier to believe this person had probably not recognized me in the wheelchair that day in the hospital. It does not matter what she thinks, it matters more what I choose to think, that I forgave her, and most of all that her reactions did not negatively affect my self-perception.

I chose to not confront her because there was nothing to gain, only the possibility of hurting or embarrassing her. Instead, I choose to believe that on that day she had seen a stranger reaching out to her and did not know how to react. By choosing not to personalize this incident and viewing it as a life lesson, I have the power to not let others' reactions crush me.

It is better when I stay on the high road, to give the benefit of the doubt when appropriate and to work at forgiving. Life is so much more peaceful when I do this. This experience reminds me to be cautious in my interpretations of events and if I can't bring myself to give others the benefit of the doubt, then forgiveness is all that is left to do.

The fourth event happened several years ago when I was at a grocery store. A checkout clerk inquired what had happened to my left hand and arm elbow-bent against my abdomen while I struggled with my right hand to pull out my bank card from my purse. Her perplexed look to my answer gave me the sense that she wondered how I could say, with a smile, that I'd had a paralyzing stroke. I then added, "I'm so glad I didn't die and I'm grateful to be alive." The grocery clerk smiled and her eyes expressed relief as though she thought my life was not over and I could still find enjoyment in it. I wanted to leave her with the idea that life can be good in spite of what happens.

Whenever I felt someone had those thoughts, I would automatically say, "I'm so lucky to be alive. I'm here and that's what counts." I would even say to someone I knew, "Life is even more precious when you have a near-death experience." These comments usually invited them to then respond positively and even take note of my positive attitude as a good way to live. I often saw people's expressions change from pity to relief and sometimes disbelief. Influencing shifts in people's thinking is enough for me to believe I have many purposes on earth.

I recall people's comments, "Why you? You don't deserve this! You are so young! It's not fair! Things like this shouldn't happen to good, young people like you!" Many people viewed the stroke as unfair, a curse. Then, there were the comments "God's trying to teach you something." "This is a warning to slow down and do less." I would agree my body sent me a strong signal that it had had enough.

I needed to have balance, to be less driven and to slow down, but I also always believed these were not the essential reasons why I had had a paralyzing stroke.

Although I knew these comments came from places of love—and possibly of fear, I still felt judged. I was extremely vulnerable at that time, so when I couldn't muster the mental energy to ignore those comments, I thought God was punishing me. In those moments, I would almost succumb to the temptation to bow my head, be sad, and lament, "Yes, poor me!" When I let myself chime in this way, I quickly lost hope.

If I couldn't steer those conversations in positive directions, once alone, I cried and found all sorts of reasons to be sad. However, when I could maintain focus and trust that good would come from this, I remembered that God is loving and merciful. I could then smile to my visitors and declare, "Well, that's life. I'm just so glad to be alive!" This upbeat and deliberate reply kept me fixed on the positive experiences throughout recovery. Our exchanges of energy became positive rather than dwelling on the pessimistic "whys."

The easiest way for me to keep conversations hopeful and life giving was to maintain a genuine smile and make any comments positive ones. Visitors had the choice to think I was unusual, in denial, or heavily medicated—or, to see it as my coping style. My consistently cheerful and positive encounters showed these people not to worry about my perspective.

This mindset prepared me to hear my friend Stella's opinion. She presented me with an enlightening perspective about my stroke. She suggested the stroke had not been strictly intended for my education but had happened also as an opportunity for others to learn and grow, too. Contrary to others' interpretations, this positive viewpoint encouraged me. It had come at a time when I needed it most. As always, Stella's gems of wisdom are timely and powerful. Every time she repeated her interpretation of my stroke with conviction, I was more comforted. The thought that others could gain from my tribulation made me feel less alone in my journey; and God was there with me, supporting me. I felt even more loved, not punished. It sealed the hope that there was indeed a divine plan in it.

My Family's Reactions to My Changed Role

The reality of my physical losses was never more intensified than when I was at home and repeatedly witnessing all the things I could no longer do for my family. From my weekend visits home to when I moved back two months after Club Rehab, I soon saw that I could not meet many of my family's needs. I couldn't prepare a meal, wash my daughter's hair and make her a ponytail, or drive my son to soccer. Seeing Louis doing all this with the help of my mother and my children deepened my sense of helplessness. I worried that my children would view me as an inadequate parent; no longer reliable. It wasn't until nine months after the discharge that I was able to help make simple meals, help with sorting laundry, or have the energy to interact minimally with my family.

In June 2005, my son was spending more time at home during the school day while preparing for his high-school final exams. One day, he told me he had developed a newfound respect for me. He saw all the therapy I did in a day, how much energy it demanded of me, and how difficult it was for me to do a chore. He explained that he finally understood why I slept on the couch every afternoon. Before this insight, he had thought I slept the entire day away. After his new awareness, he stopped commenting on my much-needed daily rest periods.

What is Normal?

The hospital was a world that provided me shelter from out there. We, the patients, were in the majority and I suspect this environment shaped for us a sense of normalcy. After weekend visits with my family, I couldn't wait to get back to the hospital. The ward was the only place where I felt normal. This idea hadn't struck me until one Sunday morning while getting ready for church while on a weekend pass.

Chloé was demonstrating less enthusiasm about dealing with my physical dilemmas. The novelty to help Louis get me up, wash me, dress me and feed me before going out had expired that Sunday morning. This little girl who had always exhibited strong maternal instincts was no longer pleased with pretending that I was a life-size doll. She asked me, "Maman, when are you going to be normal again?"

My heart cried for my child who had experienced so many losses at such a young age. I surmised my response would be crucial in helping her accept and move past this difficult situation. By some grace, my brain synapses fired on cue and I answered in a matter-of-fact way, without excuses, "This is normal for me now." I did not want her to think it was unacceptable to be this way. She looked so sad and disappointed, I wanted to cry and say to myself, poor me. Instead, I kept my deep sadness for my loss hidden deep inside me and confidently answered with a soft smile, "I will get better over time." I wanted to reassure her that caring for me physically was enough. I didn't want her, or Louis, to feel responsible for me emotionally. I especially did not want Chloé to think that my physical status was something to be shameful of, depressed about or abnormal. It also helped the situation that Louis had a positive attitude and echoed to Chloé what I had told her. I then set out to teach Chloé and Christian that what appeared to be no longer normal could be a new normal if we chose to accept loss and move forward with grace and hope.

What is normal? Most of us define normal based on our own experiences, beliefs and mindsets and this explains why what it is normal to one person may not seem normal to another. Now, when I experience loss from adversity and nothing seems normal anymore, I know it's time to redefine normal. I begin from a place in my soul where there is acceptance of the present situation and then I trust that with hard work, a healthy mindset, and commitment on my part, this too shall pass.

I needed to develop a new belief about what was normal and to accept that how I'd function in the roles of mother and wife would be different for my family and me. However, before I could even begin to think about these roles, I had to first learn and figure out how to care for myself. Then I'd be ready to focus on these two roles because they were the most important to me.

The Power in Controlling My Reactions

Venturing out into public places such as malls and restaurants in a wheelchair on my weekend and evening passes with family and friends was difficult. I ignored people's stares and reminded myself that I was an average person in an average wheelchair. I rationalized that people stared because they were amazed to see a young person in a wheelchair, one who did not look as though she belonged there. Maybe this was not true, but it worked for me. If I saw fear in their eyes, I told myself they were afraid that perhaps they could not be as brave as I was. Maybe this was not true, but it worked for me. This way of thinking helped me avoid feelings of sadness and shame. Over time, I began to see in their eyes compassion and kindness instead of fear, curiosity and pity.

Chloé, on the other hand, struggled to ignore other kids staring at her on our grocery shopping trips. One day, I understood so well why she occasionally resisted Louis's requests to push my wheelchair in public. Sometimes, he needed her to push me in my wheelchair despite my best efforts to use my one functional arm while he was pushing a shopping cart. At that point, she'd succumb to pushing me around even though other kids stared at her. I was so moved to see how this little girl learned to be so strong at such a young age. I admired her courage. She embraced this awkwardness with grace and a positive attitude. She never behaved toward me with shame or resentment. Nor did it appear to me she ever pretended that I wasn't her mother, except for one occasion that I observed she was tempted to do so.

Observing Chloé, revealed that my hemiplegia forced her to cope with her life issues prematurely. Despite this, her positive outlook and interactions with others and with me, inspired me to be truly committed to having a positive attitude. My kids were then, and continue to be, the best motivators for my trying to maintain positive actions, behaviors and words.

In the spring of 2005, I became preoccupied with what I would wear in the hot summer ahead. If I wore shorts, I would draw more attention to my limping and my AFO (ankle foot orthotic) that covered my leg below my knee. No doubt, wearing shorts while sporting an AFO would cause stares. So, I rationalized that people would then know why I limped so badly and would stop asking me what happened to my leg. It then seemed silly to worry about how I would look in shorts or skirts. Why hide it with long pants and be uncomfortably warm? Wearing an AFO was now who I was.

When I opted for seasonal comfort wear, I decided to hide my awkwardness with the unfashionable AFO behind my reliable armor of smiles and to walk with confidence. Some people still asked me how I hurt my leg and comment that it looks painful. I always interact in kind ways and politely answer all questions with a cheerful smile. I have made it my mission as a person with a disability to demonstrate that we can be whole, happy people despite any aid device in tow. I also hope it will influence any mindset out there that people with disabilities can't be happy.

Sadly, I observed that my children had some difficulty ignoring people's stares. For example, in July 2005, Christian, who was 16 at the time, drove Chloé and me to the pool for her swimming lesson. As we were returning to our car, both he and I noticed a young, pretty woman in a short skirt and fancy boots staring at me with a notable expression of disgust. He immediately shared with me his anger toward her.

I reacted in a way that I hoped taught my kids it wasn't worth wasting a second of energy feeling hurt or angry. I explained. "It's okay. She was probably frightened by the thought of ever having to wear an AFO."

He did not seem to like it that I was unfairly judged. Maybe it was because he knew that if I had the choice, I would have been wearing my fashionable shoes.

My AFO was the perfect opportunity to model to my children that I don't see myself as disabled or unsightly and should never feel shameful about any assistive device.

I am grateful for those experiences that teach me that normal does not mean we all have to be the same. This understanding gave me the license to go places and do things despite the risk of stares, judgment or pity. On that note, this helped me address my lifelong issue of hiding my flabby arms because I thought they were too big. Not anymore. Near death and hemiparesis put flabby arms into perspective. Now, I'm glad I *have* arms, full as they are, one fully active and the other just happy to be hanging around with my hand I aptly name Princess Hand. I also hoped that being comfortable with who I am would, in some way, help others feel comfortable in the presence of persons with disabilities.

My reactions to people's comments or actions determine how they affect me. I suppose my hospital visitors were in some way right when they said that God was teaching me a lesson. Although it was not their idea of lessons to be learned, they were undeniably valuable opportunities for growth and for molding healthy outlooks.

In my physiotherapy programs, I observed other patients in my situation who were overwhelmed by the physical demands of recovery and were impatient with their physical progress. Some of them even resisted the advice of therapists by stubbornly refusing to try new exercises or making excuses as to why they couldn't do it. Others did not do their homework exercises and most of these patients eventually lost hope in their recovery and gave up because improvements were slow and small. In these cases, by no fault of their own, some therapists lost interest in their clients by either not being as motivated as they might have been or by interpreting the client's lack of cooperation as a loss of interest in achieving more recovery. Unfortunately, in these cases, the patients lost more than hope, they were discharged from the program. This was very disturbing. Those needing therapy had sabotaged their chances for recovery. If only those patients could have seen that they had the power to affect change in their lives. In the end, they had robbed themselves of the opportunity to gain more recovery and improve the quality of their lives. Had they been receptive and patient enough to try different exercises and activities, they would have received positive results and boosted their confidence toward trying more.

You Reap What You Sow

Watch your thoughts; they become words.
Watch your words; they become actions.
Watch your actions; they become habits.
Watch your habits; they become character.
Watch your character; it becomes your destiny.
—Frank Outlaw

"You reap what you sow." Until my stroke, this quote always had negative connotations for me. In grade school, one of my religion instructors taught us that the meaning of "you reap what you sow" is you pay for the consequences of your bad actions. Maybe this person had mentioned you will benefit from your good actions, too, but I didn't hear it because I was too busy thinking about myself and everyone else who had to pay for all their bad acts.

This quote also confused me. When some people hurt others they did not appear to have had any remorse or consequences relative to the pain they had caused. In these cases, I felt they escaped paying their dues for hurting me or others unfairly. They didn't seem to suffer like I did. In my young adult years, I thought it was unfair how some people never seemed to pay the price for what they had done. My youth's lack of wisdom blinded me from realizing that people do indeed reap what they sow without it always being blatantly obvious to observers.

As I wrote this, I thought of the Charles Dickens character, Ebenezer Scrooge, in *A Christmas Carol*. Aside from the moral to be kind to others, I thought the story represented the importance of healing our hurts so we don't project them onto others. Scrooge's unresolved bitterness and anger manifested in his lack of compassion for the hardship and cruelty he inflicted on family members and employees. When he was faced with what he had sowed, he could heal his heart and soul, be motivated to change his ways of relating with those dearest to him and make amends.

Sometimes, it may appear that someone is not remorseful or regretful about their hurtful acts. I have two thoughts on this. They might be so enmeshed in their denial about their negative contributions that they are blinded to seeing the pain they cause. Or, they are unaware how their negative and hurtful behaviors are driven by an unhealed or unresolved issue hurting others and possibly themselves.

I have heard people say about others how the punishment did not always fit the crime. How do we know this for sure? In my opinion, a tortured soul can be more excruciating than an external punishment such as a loss of property or a job. A tortured soul might not live in peace for a long time, possibly even until death. A life in absence of peace, a tormented soul, is a painful sentence to serve. So, is it fair to surmise that someone is not reaping what they sowed?

How do I know someone is not having difficulty to live with what they've done or paying the price in some way? Or, might not their suffering be at such a deep level that their retribution is not visible? I don't know, and truthfully it is not my concern. It is between that person and their higher power. I believe it is important to forgive people so resentments are not harbored, or ill will wished for. This might return to the judging person in the form of bad karma. It is better to wish a person well.

Karma

In my quest for understanding the soul, I have learned about karma, an Indian belief that stems from ancient times and which is similar to the expression "you reap what you sow." Karma is about the choices we make to bring good to others and to the earth. There is the law of good karma as well as the law of bad karma.

Good Karma

Karma happens when a person does a good or bad deed; he/she will receive the like in return. Kindness and good deeds without self-serving motivation beget blessings. Hurtful and dishonorable behaviors beget consequences relative to the actions: misfortunes. The blessings or debts to pay might be immediate or not, and might be obvious or subtly disguised.

One of my inspirational teachers explained that karma is like a bank account: The more good deeds we do, the more blessings we will receive; the more harmful deeds we do, the relative debts we will have to pay.

I began to experience firsthand the benefits of good karma. I guess all the times we gave money, food, support and volunteered our time have all been investments in our good karmas. For example, many people we knew and hardly knew gave us prepared meals and so much more after the stroke. I was awed by the generosity of so many people and was even equally awestruck to hear people say it's because Louis or I had been good to them.

We were blessed with five months of delicious, prepared meals from my colleagues. Louis's staff collected a munificent amount of money in excess of $600 to help us defray the costs of preparing our home and purchasing the equipment for my recovery. When I look back, Louis and I often gave money in the past to worthy causes and to people in need. These gestures rewarded us with money when we needed it. How wonderful life is when you receive blessings at the time you need it most.

Service and Tithing

The same inspirational teacher taught me that service and tithing is a wonderful way to build good karma. If you give service, you will receive service, and if you tithe money, you will receive money. Most importantly, she also taught me that it is also possible to reverse bad karma. She explained that when you want to reverse bad karma, you must tithe or do service for the good of others without the expectation of a reward. She also stated that the tithe or service should be relative to the offense. This made me appreciate even more how God is merciful and forgiving by giving us ways to reverse bad karma.

This wise teacher also explained that when you tithe money, it is helpful to bless it for the goodness of others. She added that it is equally important to ask in return for abundance and prosperity. This seemed odd to me because as a Catholic I was taught that when you give, you do not ask for anything in return. This inspirational teacher explained that in order to tithe, you needed money to keep tithing, so in blessing your offerings by asking for prosperity and abundance, you can continue to tithe and give generously. Her explanation helped me to make these requests guilt-free.

Is It Karma or Not?

You might wonder what I did to reap my physical disabilities if you are thinking of the law of karma. I'm confident that I'm not paying a debt. The stroke was part of my life's divine mission, my sacred contract. I know the stroke was not a debt to pay because if it were, I would not have received all the blessings of love, money, prepared food, gifts, insight, and opportunities to give back and to share my story. I do, however, believe that if I had chosen to be bitter about my losses and had behaved with bitterness and anger, these actions would have led to a grim outcome. In that case, I would have no doubt reaped what I had sown through lack of support, and negative interactions with family, friends and healthcare providers.

I respect my life and others' lives too much to think or wish upon anyone, harmful or negative experiences. One of my purposes on earth is to share my story. My stroke was not a debt to pay, but a ticket to discover divine purpose and meaning.

Grieve to Achieve
Acceptance and Peace

God grant me the serenity to accept the things I cannot change,
courage to change the things I can, and wisdom to know the
difference.—(The Serenity Prayer) Reinhold Niebuhr

The Dalai Lama explains in his book, *The Power of Compassion*, that it is beneficial to be realistic about the circumstances of unfortunate things in our lives. Investigating how to overcome them can make us stronger and increase our self-confidence and self-reliance. Therefore, the events can be sources of inner strength. [The Dalai Lama, 1995] I believe many of my life-altering events, tragic or not, were catalysts for uncovering inner strengths. When I prevailed over the losses, these events ensued. I somehow always became a better person.

If you look at only what is, you might never attain what could be.
—Anonymous

The stroke taught me that the sooner I stopped harping on what I wanted, the sooner I could stop this negative, internal behavior and take the bull by the horns. At the time of my stroke, not letting go of what my life had been, sent me down a path of despair, doubt, pain and even more suffering. The only way I could get past this was to pray every day and tell myself I had to work hard in physiotherapy and occupational therapy. I also reminded myself to not only entertain positive thoughts but to seek the good in others and from the events of the day. Most importantly, I tried to keep a healthy perspective on grieving emotions. I allowed myself to feel anger, sadness or any grieving emotions and when they became too intense and scared me, I offered them to God instead of dwelling on them.

I've come to understand that in the beginning of grieving any loss, it is very difficult to see and appreciate the small gifts of grace, hope, kindness, and GEMS. I knew that coming to terms with the stroke losses was going to be a severe process and that I could not do it on my own. I needed the support and love of those close to me and most of all faith in God. Acceptance and peace eventually came to my rescue through prayer, meditation, and through setting intentions and actions. I did experience moments and days of doubt and anger but by the grace of God, I rarely experienced over-extended grieving periods.

As notable psychologist and author Elizabeth Kubler-Ross learned through surviving the Holocaust, there are five stages of grieving. They are: denial, anger, depression, bargaining, and acceptance. There is no sequence or particular order in which someone experiences these and each can be revisited. [Elizabeth Kubler-Ross, 1969]

The drafting of the manuscript for this book took me into my eighth year post stroke. The benefit of this is that my continued interest in learning from inspirational speakers, and authors has helped me to clarify many unclear passages and ideas in my manuscript. For example, Iyanla Vanzant on Oprah's "Life Class" series in Toronto talked about dealing with painful emotions. She urges us to, "Feel it.

Deal with it. And heal it... Until you heal the wounds of your past, you will continue to bleed. You can bandage the bleeding with food, with alcohol, with drugs, with work, with cigarettes, with sex, but eventually, it will all ooze through and stain your life. You must find the strength to open the wounds, stick your hands inside, pull out the core of the pain that is holding you in your past, the memories, and make peace with them." [Iyanla Vanzant, 2012] From what I understand, feel it means you don't bury the emotion, to deal with it is to allow yourself to experience it. And once you've done that, you are ready to heal it. These phrases reinforce to me how important it is to let ourselves go through all the stages of grieving when we experience loss. It's not wise to stay in denial, for example, because by not moving through all the other stages of grieving you never get to heal the loss.

Denial

Denial was the first stage I experienced in my grieving. In a course of a lifetime, there are many life challenges that can send a person into denial. My most significant denial was the diagnosis of hemiplegia. I was shocked when I couldn't roll over or sit up in bed. Unable to move half my body as I willed, I was flooded with confusion, and fear. Days passed and as soon as I saw that hemiplegia had invaded my body like a parasite, I secretly refused to believe it was true. I was convinced that everyone was wrong, including the doctors. I persuaded myself that I'd prove them wrong in a week. How wrong *I* was! Moreover, there was no running from this! Then it was two, three weeks and finally one month later and I could no longer deny that I was hemiplegic.

As I stayed in denial, it scared me how this manifested in poisonous thoughts and feelings. Weeks went by before I could get past the denial and think about how I was going to refurbish my damaged body. Once I accepted my condition, I began to accept that I was hemiplegic and needed therapy.

However, once in therapy I went into denial again. One long rehab gymnasium wall was lined with low, large, flatbed tables of multiple persons lying on them, persons with missing limbs trying to learn how to sit up and walk again. Everyone there was clearly in need of therapy—but why me. After all, I still had all my body parts. Again, I began to think that my paralysis was temporary. It took several visits before I could see that I needed to be there. Basic hand, arm, foot, knee, leg, and hip movements were impossible. Reality finally sank in.

Somewhat educated on the stages of grief, I knew I couldn't ignore any of them and had to live through this experience of denial. But, I also knew that to live through it in a healthy way was going to help me get to the next stage of grieving—whichever one that was going to be. Thereafter, every time I revisited denial, it was less intense and more short-lived.

Today, denial still comes back to test me. For example, I often decline to accept help when it's obvious to everyone but me that I need their assistance in completing a task. I want to prove to myself that I can do simple tasks with my hands involving fine motor skills or, sometimes, large motor skills. My sister-in-law, Ivy, tactfully brought to my attention how my stubbornness about not accepting help was adding to my challenges. Observations like this are so much easier to swallow and accept when it's delivered in as loving and kind a way as Ivy did. She helped me see how my pride interfered with the acceptance of my limitations and the receiving of others' help. Had I been criticized in a judgmental tone, I know myself well enough to know that I might have stayed in denial about this a lot longer than would have been good for me.

Anger

During the first weeks in the rehab hospital, I needed to blame someone or something for my stroke. Anger cleverly distracted me from the reality of my condition, and it was the best I could do to make sense of my hemiplegia. Eventually, I came to my senses and chose to change my thoughts when I saw another patient have a wonderful attitude about his permanently broken body from a suicide attempt. I surely could cope better with my situation by finding healthier ways. The thoughts and feelings associated with anger showed me that although it was okay to experience it for a while, I needed to move on.

I first needed to understand what precisely angered me. There was the anger related to my physical losses and my roles as a functional human being. I could no longer fully function as I used to as a mother, wife, teacher, community member, friend, aunt, sister, and daughter. I hated that I couldn't walk up the stairs in my house to tuck my 6-year-old daughter into bed.

When my emotional incontinence was well into the crying phase, I cried alone, and with Louis, many tears for the life I'd once had. There was a deep sense of loss preceding helplessness and accompanied by anger. These feelings worsened when people tried to cheer me up and tell me others had it worse than I did. This made me feel as though they wanted me to deny or bury my feelings about my reality. I know that family and friends meant well, but for me, at that time, I needed listeners, not cheerleaders. I felt as though I was pushed not to feel my pain, and these comparisons minimized my pain and loss. Pain is pain and loss is loss no matter what size it comes in. I didn't want cheerleaders, but people to listen to me. Acknowledging my pain on my own made it easier to live with.

I needed to allow myself to grieve what once was so I could begin to face what was ahead. Who knew what was ahead? No one. I knew what I had lost in mobility but didn't know what I would regain. So I couldn't even aspire and hold onto future possibilities because the unknown and uncertainty of the future was so frightening that I was tempted to stay in the anger stage of grieving. But if I wanted any chance of a decent new life, I needed to let go of the anger and move on. I needed to let go of blame so I could accept who I had become.

Today, I no longer have any anger but I do get frustrated when my invisible disabilities compromise my relationships. When an emotionally upsetting event occurs, the part of the brain that used to kick in and could reason logically to choose an appropriate response, often no longer does. I get overwhelmed in my head. It's like I'm in a big room filled with filing cabinets and the answers of what to say and do are lost somewhere in the countless drawers. I'm running from one to the other in a rush but discover they're all locked. So I fish in my memories for a similar situation and then realize I don't know what words to use. By then, in a fluster, I blurt out an emotional response that infuses the situation which usually backfires and all parties are burned. I get angrier with myself because I've lost the ability to be in control of my emotions and thoughts. This anger is further expressed in ways that leave others feeling I'm angry with them, when actually, I'm upset with myself.

Time and distance from the situation help me to gain a clearer perspective of what I experienced. Once I better understand the emotion by practicing CBT, I can discuss and process the event with the person involved. It's as though intense emotions and feelings take a long detour before my brain can identify and understand my associated thoughts. When these delays occur, this prevents me from clearly and calmly processing the event without confusion. Sometimes, my brain functions quite well, like it used to in these types of situations, but this deceives me into thinking I'm healed—until the next time my brain malfunctions. These surprises get me frustrated with myself and with people who don't understand what it's like. A sense of helplessness and incompetency hits me so hard that I feel sad and regretful. A lot of work then goes into self-forgiveness and making amends.

Acceptance

It was not an easy feat to accept my limitations and the realities of my disabilities. In fact, no loss is easy to accept! When I lost independence in self-care and mobility, I was entirely dependent on others to dress me, take me to the washroom, and place me in a wheelchair or into bed. Self-pity was so easy that I knew I used it as a cop-out to avoid working on moving past my grief. Therefore, I ordered myself to suck it up and channel my anger to find new, healthy ways to grieve. These weren't clear to me but I was determined to find them!

I still allowed myself to openly express regrets of loss to my family and friends. However, if I wanted their ongoing support and understanding I did so in ways that would not cause them more worries about me. Expressing regret didn't mean lamenting. I also decided that using statements with hope of what I will someday do again and to express regret with a twist of humor, such as "Oh darn, I can't wait to pull up my own pants someday!" would avoid lamenting about what I couldn't do anymore. Reframing statements with a positive slant had a profound effect on my attitude and outlook.

The big, instantaneous recovery was not in my destiny. I instinctively knew my road of recovery to regain functions and movements would be slow, small, and in unpredictable increments. Therefore, I asked God to bless me with the courage to face what was, the strength to accept it, the discernment to know how to do it, and everything else I needed to live it gracefully. In good time, I found that I was appreciative of all the GEMS—a muscle twitch, the first footstep, the love and support of family and friends, all the things I had, and living in a country where the medical expenses were paid.

Once I allowed myself to see the blessings of my new life, the healing process began and it was easier to let go of my old life, the anger and the blame. I replaced the temptations to look back at what life was like by focusing on the GEMS I received and the outcomes I desired. Accepting a new life meant setting small, attainable goals. It was important to know that each small goal would lead to my final goals of walking and using my left hand again. Every victory helped me to believe that my physical limitations were temporary. I adopted the attitude that every new day has infinite possibilities and to be receptive for this.

Shifting Thoughts of Anger and Blame to Acceptance and Peace

The paralyzing stroke, initially, caused my life to spin out of control. When my anger shot its arrow of blame, it targeted my teaching career. I obsessed about how the years of a demanding teaching profession had contributed to my stroke.

Weakness of attitude becomes weakness of character.
—Anonymous

Evidently, my sour inner world simmered in rising anger and disappointment that was not congruent with my desires for living positive thoughts. This awareness helped me realize that my negative thoughts about blaming, provoked more anger. Those thoughts were going to be harmful for my whole well-being. I was seeing a future me characterized as a bitter stroke survivor. This unflattering image scared me into re-thinking about who I wanted to be: a peaceful, positive, and hopeful person.

My colleagues who visited me might have noticed this and I certainly didn't want to affect them with my garbage. I am grateful for the insight to recognize that I had to change my thought patterns. I was very much aware that expressing negative feelings or thoughts blocked or poisoned my opportunities for continued inner growth and recovery. It was also beginning to cloud my seeing and the appreciation of the many minor victories in my recovery at that time. All this prompted me to search for ways to restore a healthy emotional state of mind about my career.

I subconsciously made a mental shift in my thoughts from the negative (anger, and blame) to the positive (gratitude and attitude). An inward acknowledgement of all the love, support, and visits from all my colleagues helped me to refocus on appreciating the aspects in my professional life that had made me feel happy, blessed, and hopeful. In doing this, my actions and feelings redirected my life in a productive, positive, and healthy direction.

I finally accomplished this when I thought of my students and how dear they were to me. I had previously taught half of them in grade three where we had developed a special bond through the sharing and processing of many challenges and the loss of a student's parent from a terminal illness. Only on rare occasions had I ever experienced such a profound, heartfelt connection with a whole class! As for the other half of my class, I got to know them enough in the three weeks of school before the stroke to initiate and have a close bond, which is why all the students in my class are still dear to me and I often think of them.

The thought of missing out on the privilege of finishing the school year with these students filled me with deep sadness—another loss. Cherishing my students began to rekindle a positive perspective about my work. Quickly, the negative blaming thoughts toward my profession dissipated but the sadness and probable loss of a career did creep in. For the remainder of the school year, visiting my students and receiving their on-going cards decorated with colorful words of love and support helped me digest this reality.

In June 2005, I considered myself truly blessed when my students presented me with a beautifully handcrafted quilt they'd made with love and the assistance of a colleague and friend, Elvira. Even though I was unable to teach them grade five, they had shown me that we were connected at a precious, intimate level. I am fortunate that I did not have a new group of students because the three weeks of September would not have been enough time to create a bond like the one I had with my special class.

I felt further blessed when colleagues from other schools with whom I had taught in my school division performed thoughtful, loving gestures. They provided prepared meals for my family for several months, visited me in the hospital and at home, generously gave gifts that I cherish to this day, and they prayed with me, and for me.

Depression

I had no control over the dramatic changes in my life but I did have control over how I would react to it. The temptation to hate my current situation and what I looked like always seemed to be lurking in the crevices of my mind to accompany every difficult struggle. Scared of how deep I'd fall when vulnerable to these thoughts, I purposely sought out the people I knew would remind me of my strengths so I could refocus my hope for the future.

I hated that my body couldn't move as I wanted it to. I needed someone to pull me up out of bed and position my body back in bed. I hated waiting for a care provider in the hospital to take me to the washroom and that I had to wait longer than others because I refused to have a male take me to the washroom. I had started my period three days after the stroke and if my husband had never tended to my toileting care, I'd be damned if another man would begin.

I resented that I had to learn how to sit up again and perform so many other basic movements that I'd already learned as a baby and a toddler. All this seemed justifiable to allow me to detest my life. I felt this way until I observed that negativity slowly lead to despair, and more disappointing anger.

At that time in my grieving phase, I cried at anything. Fortunately, this part of my emotional incontinence didn't last too long. I didn't know it then but I was depressed. Depression is common after any loss and especially when there is an acquired brain injury as I had sustained. Even singing, which had previously always brought me joy, made me cry, not because I could no longer sing but because my sadness was so intense.

For several months after the stroke, watching a sentimental scene on TV, even a commercial or hearing a heartwarming story, would provoke uncontrollable sobbing. These moments of crying actually commiserated with my deep despair of loss. I suspected I was experiencing a chemical imbalance so had to admit that this situation was beyond what I could handle. I could no longer ignore those persistent, intense, dark, solemn feelings, so I saw my family doctor. This difficult time wasn't like it had been in the past when I could overcome it by solely relying on my inner strengths. Knowing I had never before experienced a depression of this intensity, I accepted the taking of antidepressants and within three days I was able to crawl out of this darkness.

In fact, the medication worked so well that I couldn't cry during the seven years I took it except for once because of the shocking event of a family member's crisis. Once I stopped taking the antidepressants, it took almost a year before strong emotions could motivate tears. Now, I can cry again and am in control of my tears.

Bargaining

As far back as I can remember, I tended to bargain in difficult situations. If I did my best to please others, I would win them over and resolve any issues. The downside of this was that I usually compromised more than the other person and later felt resentful. Most often, bargaining didn't work because what I hadn't realized was that I needed to find within myself what I needed to change in me, not how I could influence others to do what I wanted.

When I was in hospital, I negotiated with the hospital staff that I would be ready to be discharged once I learned how to walk up and down steps one foot at a time. When that time came, I wasn't ready to leave. Somehow, I had convinced myself that on discharge day, I would not need the wheelchair and would walk out with a cane. This bargaining had set me up for the greatest fall I ever experienced. I cried all the way home because I was devastated that I needed to be wheeled out of the hospital and would need to use the wheelchair at home.

Like many women, I love my shoes. I was never a runner-wearing woman and hated that I had to wear runners everywhere the first year post stroke. It took years before I could actually give away all the cherished, high-heeled shoes in my closet, with the exception of a couple pairs in case some day by some miracle I could wear them. That I can now wear sturdy heels less than two inches high is a compromise for not being able to wear high-heeled shoes again. I stopped buying these coveted shoes seven years after my stroke when my ankle would twist or I would trip as I unsteadily test-walked them around the house. I stopped thinking that no longer wearing my big AFO did not mean that I would someday be able to wear high-heeled shoes. I reminded myself where I started from and traded bargaining for high-heels with accepting to be content wearing shoes with a slight heel and a hidden shoe orthotic insert.

I bargained with myself about the capabilities of my compromised physical abilities. My false sense of ability was misleading where my AFO was concerned. I hoped it would enable my walking abilities to closely match those of the average person. I thought it equipped me to walk almost like everyone else. My pride seemed to be at the root of pushing my body to walk fast and far as I tried to prove to others I could keep up with them. Until six years post stroke, I was still in denial about being hemiparetic and would go on leisure walks and try to keep up with everybody.

One time, a friend marveled at how well I was doing and stubborn as I was, I kept walking even though I knew I was walking too fast and for too long. I paid the price with hip tendon injuries that took well beyond two years to heal. To this day, these tendons are sensitive and vulnerable to re-injury.

I've learned to avoid hiking my right hip up to overcompensate for my left leg, as well as make sure I properly lift my upper left thigh and flex my left foot up as I step onto my heel while everting my left foot. Now, when I walk with someone, I've learned how to think of doing these movements while carrying on a simple conversation. However, I'm exhausted after these walks and have to rest.

Bargaining for normal body movements proved to be a physically harmful and disappointing experience. Now, instead, I try to be aware of what I want to accomplish and avoid bargaining by setting realistic and attainable goals. I try not to depend on external forces to get what I want, but on internal strengths.

Insights to My Approach in Recovery and Adversity

I first thought about the meaning of my existence when I was an adolescent. I viewed the essence of my existence as a physical body, which was like a suitcase encasing my soul. Since then, I have come to understand I am not a physical being with soul, I am soul incarnated in my physical body coexisting with all my other bodies. My soul is eternal and it is visiting here on earth in this body.

I'm a visual person. Therefore, I decided to explain my understanding of my existence by visually representing my view of how and why we are more than just a physical body, and how we need to be attentive to all our bodies to achieve harmony and happiness. Diagram B shows each body in its own circle.

As life continues to teach me new insights about my existence, my ideas on this topic are ever evolving and my view becomes more fine-tuned. Therefore, what I offer you here is my best understanding thus far. I share what I have come to understand and hope it might be helpful to someone to recognize why it is important to pay attention to all his or her bodies and not just his/her physical body.

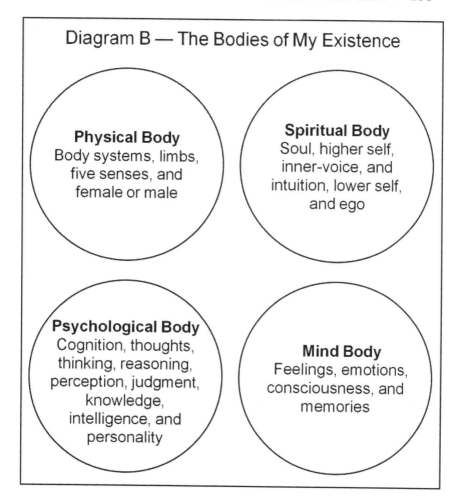

Diagram B — The Bodies of My Existence

Physical Body
Body systems, limbs, five senses, and female or male

Spiritual Body
Soul, higher self, inner-voice, and intuition, lower self, and ego

Psychological Body
Cognition, thoughts, thinking, reasoning, perception, judgment, knowledge, intelligence, and personality

Mind Body
Feelings, emotions, consciousness, and memories

The Physical Body

Our five senses explore and confirm the existence of our physical body. Of the four bodies, our physical body is the only tangible one.

My stroke left me completely paralyzed from my left eye to the tip of my toes. The left side of my face drooped for several weeks, my hand was an unyielding fist, and my left arm was bent in a rigid position for many months—both glued against my chest. I used a wheelchair for several months, and a cane for several more months. I also wore an ankle foot orthotic (AFO) for several years. While I regained some use of my left leg over the first few weeks, I didn't have movement in my left fingers until after one year, or functional use of my left hand until several years later. Even now, my left arm is not fully functional. I still need, and will, most likely indefinitely require a right hand signal installed on all vehicles I drive. Over the years, I have experienced additional complications as a result of my stroke, such as pulled tendons in my groin, tendonitis in both my affected and good shoulders, and injuries from tripping and falling.

Taking care of my physical body now requires me to take an anticoagulant for life. Most importantly, stroke recovery involved extensive medical treatment and many forms of physical therapy. This included mainstream therapies such as physiotherapy, occupational therapy, speech therapy, massage therapy, and chiropractic care as well as alternative health therapies such as pranic healing, acupuncture, and sacral cranial therapy. In addition, I had consultations or received services from many medical specialists, pharmacists, orthotists, nutritionists, nurses, home care workers, and alternative practitioners. In the first year following my stroke, I attended over 400 appointments, and nearly 1400 appointments in the nine years since my stroke. I have spent literally thousands of hours caring for my physical body and working to reclaim as much physical function as possible.

Maintaining a regular exercise routine has also been important to my physical recovery and overall health. Research supports that exercise helps lift one's spirit, improve one's ability to cope with stress, and maintain a healthy cardiovascular system. When I think of a time I experienced stress at home or at work, I can recall how physical activities such as gardening or going for a walk helped me feel physically stronger, emotionally better, think more clearly, and be more hopeful. This is not just a coincidence: physical exercise causes chemical processes that produce endorphins to release in the brain. Endorphins are the happy hormones; they reduce anxiety and sensitivity to pain. For me, along with exercise, it is also important to maintain a healthy diet in order to have the vitality I need to be and feel healthy.

The Psychological Body

The psychological body is the cognitive processor of information. Cognitive processes involve the mental processing of thinking, reasoning, acquiring knowledge, and forming perceptions, judgments, and thoughts, as well as developing intelligence, all of which shape one's personality.

In my case, because of my brain damage, some of my cognitive processes are compromised. I can experience trouble processing, managing and making sense of incoming information. This creates confusion and provokes all sorts of emotions. In the period immediately following my stroke, my brain also couldn't easily process written information. Even now, if I receive a written document, especially if it has complex sentences, and the information contained evokes an emotional response, I need someone to explain the letter to me.

I also can't manage too many stimuli. For instance, if I am surrounded by many conversations in a social setting, I have difficulty staying focused on one conversation, and filtering out the noise of others. My brain quickly feels overloaded. I get overwhelmed and mentally exhausted. Other psychological challenges include organizing tasks and managing my schedule. Multi-tasking continues to be a challenge with which I struggle. Over time, I have become much better at multi-tasking but have never fully recovered the ability to do so at the level I once took for granted. For instance, it took me seven years to regain the ability to comfortably engage in a simple conversation while walking. Today, I still struggle to switch between English and French when speaking. It isn't easy to find my words and physically pronounce them until my brain is comfortably immersed in the French part of my brain. Also, my mouth along with the tongue muscles need to warm up to pronounce the French words. Nine years later, I still have numbness on the left side of my mouth, as if I had seen the dentist earlier in the day.

Dealing with my cognitive challenges required me to learn and apply strategies, and this is still an ongoing process. In some cases, it meant learning memory techniques to be able to remember phone numbers, for instance. For complex cognitive processes, such as understanding and remembering complicated texts, I had to retrain my brain for comprehension by repeatedly practice-reading line by line. Still today, randomly pulling memories or information does not always happen smoothly and quickly. It seems like my brain is a confusing mess of filing cabinets with jammed drawers. This is probably why I need to maintain structure and organization in my physical environment to reduce confusion, and to spare my limited energy level from searching for things.

When emotions are engaged, I have to step back and consciously give time to identify what I am thinking. If emotions are intense, I often have to rely upon others to help me process my thoughts and understanding. Although my brain can still perform the many tasks it used to do, it just cannot do them all at once, nor as quickly and as easily as before. And that's OK.

The Mind Body

The mind body is about our emotions, feelings, and consciousness. The emotions and feelings are the outward expressions of the thoughts we create from our subjective interpretations of facts and experiences, and the meanings we attribute to them. It is not about how the brain processes information (the psychological body) but what we do with it, and how we react and work with it, along with our memories that can get enmeshed in these expressions. If we are preoccupied with thoughts then this is the opposite of being in a conscious state of presence or awareness where we experience mindfulness, and peaceful centeredness.

In my case, my stroke affected my ability to emotionally process events. Since the stroke, if I am not careful, I can easily perseverate [repeat or prolong an action, thought, or utterance after the stimulus that prompted it has ceased] on thoughts entangling me in distressing emotions and feelings. For example, my emotional incontinence caused me to react inappropriately, such as laughing when someone was hurt. I also couldn't demonstrate an appropriate emotional response of empathy for many years because these intense thoughts would not become conscious for a long while afterward, and sometimes not at all. This can still be the case today. Even now, years later, unless I take the time to deliberately process thoughts, emotions, and feelings about an experience, it can take several weeks or months before I am even aware that I am upset and have feelings associated with that experience.

I learned post-stroke from my neuropsychologist that unmet expectations only disappointed me and not the person I thought was responsible for my frustrations. Until then, I had it all backwards. I had spent my life surmising that my feelings were the result of events and people's actions in my life. It was important that I learn that thoughts manifest into emotions, and through mindful thinking, I can change unwanted feelings. This level of consciousness made me aware that I am the creator of my feelings, that I can choose not to cloud my mind with consuming thoughts.

Working with my mind body involved learning Cognitive Behavior Therapy (CBT). My stroke affected how I deal with emotions and feelings and changed how I relate with others. My family and I had to learn how to deal with my new behaviors. I wasn't just being a difficult, moody person on purpose, or by choice. Everyone had to change his or her expectations of me and learn how to interpret and not personalize my behaviors. Essential to my happiness is knowing that my emotions are not always based on facts. Upsetting or uncomfortable feelings are cues that I must first internally identify the provocative thought, and then determine if I'm reacting to fact or hypothesis, and when necessary ask others if I have accurately interpreted and understood their action or statement. Practicing CBT ensures that I live with a healthy state of mind and it positively influences my emotions and feelings, creating better memories.

The Spiritual Body

The spiritual body refers to soul, higher self, inner voice, intuition, and lower self (ego). I include lower self (ego) because once its effect on the mind is understood, this understanding serves to remind one to stop thinking, to breathe mindfully, and to be in a place of awareness. The lack of satisfaction we get from ego can also be one of the reasons that drive us to reawaken, to reconnect to soul, and to achieve a state of awareness in oneness with God.

Focusing on mindful breathing, meditation or prayer is an excellent way to be attuned to our higher self. The more I do this, the clearer becomes my inner voice. It guides me in making choices that are in the best interest of others and myself. I've learned that when I am not living a consistent routine in these practices, I become less grounded, more easily distracted from living in the now, consumed by thoughts, and become less mindful. Since the stroke, I easily experience anxiety and can now control this better if I remain faithful to daily mindfulness and prayer, as well as practice meditation regularly.

Looking back, I realize why I felt anxiety and unrest in the years before my stroke. Personal counseling, many self-help books and listening to motivational tapes were indeed beneficial but to some extent, I still felt sad, unsettled, and not whole. I now realize that anxiety, sadness, and unrest are really about compulsion—as Carolyn Myss brought to my attention in her audiobook titled, *The Language of Archetypes*. This compulsion was my soul's way of calling me to actively and daily engage with my higher self so I could stop ignoring my life's mission and get on with my life's purpose.

Carolyn Myss, in the same audio book, also suggested that if someone is in therapy and remains depressed or unhappy, it might be because their spirituality isn't an integral part of his or her therapy or counseling sessions. I cannot help but think that unaddressed spiritual problems may explain why some people continue to feel unfulfilled and uneasy in their lives. This notion confirms to me that not one of our bodies can afford to be ignored. I think it is unfortunate that many conventional counseling approaches—and therapies—focus only on the psychological, physical and/or mind dimensions of healing. The spiritual body is often excluded.

Engaging the spiritual body completes my whole approach to healing because with it, I gain awareness, meaning, and purpose. To be aware and present through prayer, mindful breathing, or meditation brings me to a peaceful state of mind. This helps me to engage in a physical task or to deal with a situation effectively, and this also generates feel-good hormones that make it easier to practice CBT. CBT alone isn't enough to help me manage my thoughts and their ensuing emotions and feelings successfully. I need to practice consciousness in what I think and do to bring me to a higher level of awareness. Taking care of my spiritual body brings the energy I need to manage all my other bodies. I feel one with God and spiritually connected to what is happening around me even when I'm dealing with difficult challenges. I feel peace knowing that all these moments too shall pass and they don't change who I am: those difficult moments are transient and I am eternal. Being spiritually connected, one with God, for me, is living with purpose.

Harmony through Interconnected Bodies

In Diagram C, the center intersection of all four bodies (with the dark musical note) represents that I am mindfully engaging all bodies as

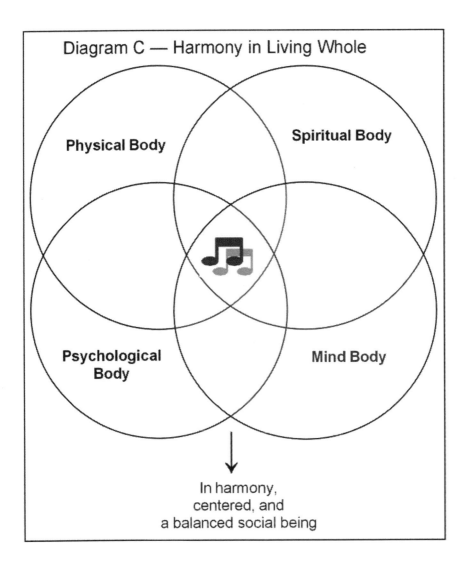

Diagram C — Harmony in Living Whole

Physical Body

Spiritual Body

Psychological Body

Mind Body

In harmony, centered, and a balanced social being

needed, all intersected. I see it as a dance choreographed masterfully with all four bodies timely stepping in and out according to the beat of my unique needs. The musical note in the center symbolizes my soul is in harmony, there is balance in my life, and I feel centered. The shadow of the musical note symbolizes that my state of mind has a positive ripple effect on my environment and social life.

If a person interconnects their four bodies uniquely to their needs he/she can live healthily and in harmony with our world. If one of these bodies is neglected, mistreated or ignored, the outcome of this can manifest as dis-ease in any or all of the other bodies. This can be in the form of physical, psychological, emotional, or spiritual ailments, discomfort, disease, or even death.

Whenever I experience discomforts or annoyances, I know I need to take better care of myself. If I ignore my spiritual body, I begin to feel stress, which reflects in my choices, surroundings and relationships. Therefore, when this happens, I know I need to return to meditating regularly. If I feel exhausted or sluggish I know I need to exercise my physical body and eat healthily. If I feel negative about others or about myself, I know I need to work on changing my thought patterns and practice more CBT.

Diagram D (next page) represents the disengagement of the physical body. This detachment creates imbalance, loss, and disharmony because of the offending circumstances. When a person isn't healthy in many ways, it is more difficult to be a positive and healthy social being. To give you an example, seven years after my stroke, I stopped meditating and exercising so fell into a rut. I had depression-like symptoms and I realized that I was spiritually starved. I needed to get back into a healthy spiritual and social routine. In this case, the spiritual body was out of harmony and disengaged. Therefore, when a body is not intersecting with the other bodies there is less, or even no, harmony.

I can think of when I observed other stroke survivors who were

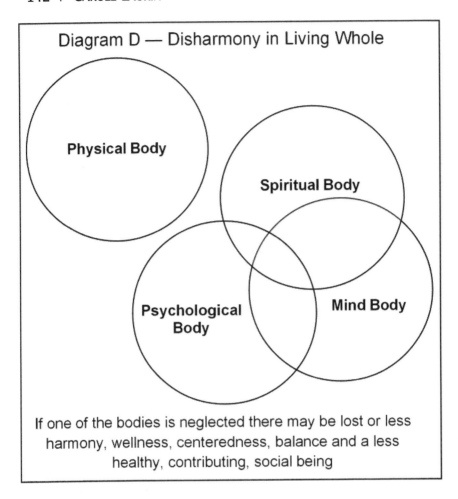

Diagram D — Disharmony in Living Whole

Physical Body

Spiritual Body

Psychological Body

Mind Body

If one of the bodies is neglected there may be lost or less harmony, wellness, centeredness, balance and a less healthy, contributing, social being

overwhelmed by their physical losses and had lost the desire to work determinedly with hope and confidence for physical recovery. Sometime into their recovery, they stopped testing the limits of their physical bodies and stopped pushing their bodies to relearn and train how to strengthen their weakened or paralyzed muscles. They appeared to have lost determination, perseverance, and self-trust so they expressed helplessness.

I believe each person has his/her own unique dance in weaving the needs of the four bodies together for acquiring harmony and peace internally, physically, and socially. What nourishes one person may not be the correct menu for the other. Each person requires appropriately suitable methods, strategies, healing modalities and tools for harmonious living. Peace can be achieved when all four bodies engage in overcoming an event, problem, or significant crisis. I know that to ignore the spiritual body invites lost faith, weakened self-trust and inner strength and more. Also, to mend my broken body, I needed all other bodies at work.

Higher Self versus Lower Self

Follow the voice of your spirit
Remember to dream
Listen to the wisdom of your soul
Dance to the music in your heart.—Anonymous

I dedicate a chapter to higher self and lower self because of their important roles in empowering my ability to make better choices. I first learned of these two concepts in the GeoTran workshops and then in pranic healing literature and workshops I've been attending since January 2005. Both prompted my quest to understand their significance and to know how best to get to and stay attuned with my higher self. Living attuned to my higher self and still aware of how my lower self tries to take control is no longer confusing and testing my relationship with God. Meditation and prayer, I have found, amplifies my higher self's voice of wisdom and my relationship with God and his divine beings.

Defining Higher Self and Lower Self

Higher self and lower self are the yin and yang of my inner dialogues. Explaining these two concepts along with their related emotions, I

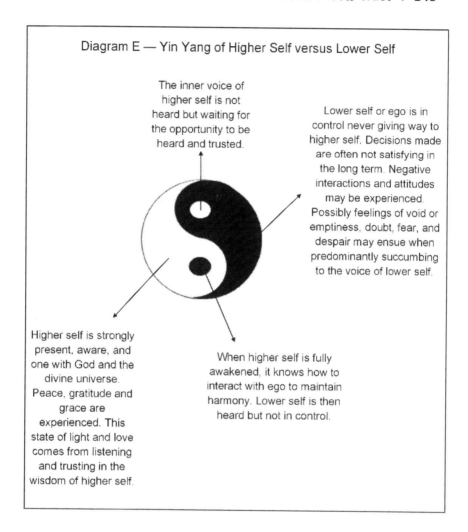

Diagram E — Yin Yang of Higher Self versus Lower Self

The inner voice of higher self is not heard but waiting for the opportunity to be heard and trusted.

Lower self or ego is in control never giving way to higher self. Decisions made are often not satisfying in the long term. Negative interactions and attitudes may be experienced. Possibly feelings of void or emptiness, doubt, fear, and despair may ensue when predominantly succumbing to the voice of lower self.

Higher self is strongly present, aware, and one with God and the divine universe. Peace, gratitude and grace are experienced. This state of light and love comes from listening and trusting in the wisdom of higher self.

When higher self is fully awakened, it knows how to interact with ego to maintain harmony. Lower self is then heard but not in control.

hope, will provide clarity in your spiritual journey as it did in mine. Higher self is the voice of my soul, an extension of God, which can also be my guardian angel, an angel's or a saint's voice, and even a divine being. If I were to describe soul to someone who is an atheist or a non-religious person, I would use the words intuition, vibes, higher being, or higher self.

Lower self is the ego and works against higher soul. I believe this because I observe the decisions that are inspired by my ego are based in desire, are reactive or self-serving, and do not benefit all involved. Therefore, it's driven to keep you in a state of wanting that never gives you lasting or permanent satisfaction. I experience lower self's motivation as the need for instant gratification. Higher self encourages me to grow in divine connection with God and lower self challenges my divine connection with God.

Diagram E (previous page) illustrates my interpretation of higher self versus lower self using the yin yang symbol. In the GeoTran workshop, one of the spiritual teachers cleverly used the yin yang symbol to explain balancing the dark and light qualities within us. This inspired me to use the yin yang symbol to explain my view of higher and lower selves.

Understanding How Emotions Affect Us and Others

My love for learning includes the hows and whys of human behaviors. Reading the books from David R. Hawkins and the renowned Japanese scientist, Masaru Emoto helped me to understand, from a quantum physics perspective, the effect of emotions' energies on our auras (also called field, energy body) and the environment. Hawkins explains how the aura is a high-frequency electrical field (also called vibrations) that surrounds a physical body and emits radiation. Kirlian photography visually proves an energy body exists by its emitted radiation. [David R. Hawkins, *Power vs Force—The Hidden Determinants of Human Behavior*, 2002] Emoto's research demonstrated how concept words and phrases have energy fields that manifest their likeness in frozen ice crystals, beautiful, unformed or distorted. [Emoto, 2004]

The photographs of Emoto's experiments convinced me that thoughts do have energies and powers that manifest from their related emotions. Consequently, these words or thoughts affect our attitudes and environments. Then, Hawkins's map of consciousness helped me understand how the relationship of high-level frequencies of emotions such as trust, optimism, forgiveness, understanding, reverence, and serenity relate to higher self. Low-level frequency emotions such as desire, hate and anxiety relate to lower self. [*ibid.*]

How much more grievous are the consequences of anger than the causes of it.—Marcus Aurelius

I have come to understand how the vibrations of our auras affect those of others. Can you recall a situation in which two people were angry, one was yelling and the other person reacted by yelling back. Did it diffuse the situation? It most likely did not. Most often, reactions of these types infuse situations with more anger. If the exchange progresses to words that are more hurtful, this may escalate into hurtful physical actions and even violence. It does not have to be a situation this extreme; verbal expressions of anger can also negatively affect others. In fact, anger, in any form has the power to negatively affect others who are either involved or not in the conflict and even the person who manifested it by it ripple effect.

This does not mean we are defenseless against others' emotions but we can consciously choose to respond from a higher vibration or emotional level. In negative situations, choosing to respond with actions of loving-kindness and compassion can diffuse lower level emotions such as anger, resentment and bitterness. Although the recipients of negative emotions are not responsible for initiating negative energy, they are accountable for how they react to it. We have the power to stop the ripple effects of negative energy by responding from higher levels, staying on the high ground so to speak.

On that note, we can also be equally responsible for breaking the positive ripple effect of high-level energies with our negative words, emotions or actions. In this case, think of a time when you consciously did not allow the anger of another person to affect you and how doing this enabled you to feel unscathed, unaffected and possibly at peace. For example, a caregiver remains calm in the face of an angry child's full tantrum. This eventually influences the child to calm down. A positive exchange of actions restores the energy flow between caregiver and child. The caregiver experiences success in creating a teachable moment for the child.

To understand better the power of emotional energies affecting one another, think of a time when you walked past a stranger and all of a sudden, you felt an unexplainable chill race through your body. Your aura sensed the negative energy emitted by that person's intense emotional state and aura. Think of a time when the entrance of a person into a room brought you feelings of joy, relaxation, elatedness, awkwardness, tension, or uncomfortable heaviness. If this person has emotions of high-level frequencies, you will experience joy and the mood in the room lightens up, inevitably affecting your mood and that of others. If this person has low-level frequencies then the atmosphere becomes tense, uncomfortable and possibly unbearable. These common situations show how our auras radiate to and affect others.

Anger or other negative emotions that spill over onto other people can have a painful, negative boomerang effect. During stroke recovery, I was aware of this instinctively and knew I had to focus on positive thoughts that would ensure I attracted positive energy and results. Without knowing it, I subconsciously knew how to work the law of attraction, "Like attracts like!" Today, my vehicles for achieving a high-level state of mind and which raise my aura's vibrational level, are meditation and the conscious choice of healthy spiritual practices and daily activities.

Living with Ears for Higher Self or Lower Self?

When I began to wise up about the powers of higher self and lower self, I realized that my lower-self voice had often competed with the higher-self voice to get my attention. It won its influence over me when my state of mind wasn't grounded and centered. Crazy as it sounds, it was as though there were two voices trying to convince me to select their viewpoint. Usually the lower was like a spoiled, whining, demanding child and the higher self was calm and clear, but confident. If I wasn't receptive to the higher self, my ego won. In these situations, I undoubtedly experienced internal conflict. I observed that my lower self had the tendency to operate from a level of fear, defensiveness and selfish survival. If I made a choice at that level, it often resulted in unsatisfying, disappointing and negative outcomes.

In the situations in which I was not receptive to the guidance of higher self, I was distracted by life itself or by the desire for instant gratification. Many times in my life before understanding this, I had danced solely to the tune of the lower self's wants. I wouldn't dare declare this as unfortunate because in hindsight, I learned why connectedness with my higher self was vital to harmonious living.

Higher self helps me view crises and traumas as opportunities to learn more about who I am, to draw from hidden strengths so I can find new meaning and purpose. In my experience, my lower self encouraged the views that crises and traumas were unfortunate tragedies that would forever keep me bogged down with negative thoughts, emotions, and attitudes. Had I remained in the company of misery and in a stagnant state of lower self, I would not have been liberated to live life full of divine opportunities and possibilities.

I understand how tempting and easy it is to give in to ego, the lower self. There are many distractions and temptations that might even seduce me away from taking the quiet time for meditation, that precious time required to hear my higher self speak or simply to remember that this part of my self is alive, and that my internal peace is dependent on an active coexistence.

Struggling to Stay Attuned to My Soul's Higher Voice

The stress of difficult challenges can make it tricky to identify which voice is the higher self or the lower self. I learned concrete strategies of how to tap into my higher self's wisdom for answers. One of the strategies was the use of muscle testing from GeoTran and the other scanning from pranic healing. At the time of the stroke, I was still learning how to use and rely on muscle testing to assist in making decisions. The stroke provided a wonderful opportunity to learn the importance of muscle testing as a way of tapping into the energy body's wisdom for decision making.

Early September 2004, I was enrolled in a university post-graduate course. A few weeks after my stroke, I wanted to withdraw from the independent study course for obvious reasons. I had enough on my plate.

Louis and Stella advised me not to be hasty in my decision. With my permission, she muscle-tested me and it revealed that I should not drop the course. I was surprised by this and not comfortable with the answer. I doubted the muscle test and allowed my ego to entertain me with ideas and thoughts that this would be too much for me to undertake. After all, I couldn't sit up on my own, so how could I write four papers and a final exam. More so, how could I do research when reading was such a tedious and demanding task, or how could I type with one hand and find the time to read, study, and write four university papers within three months on top of daily therapy? Surely, I'd fail.

Stella enlisted the help of a fellow colleague and classmate, Colleen, to communicate with the professor to extend my deadlines, for which I am very grateful. Stella then urged me to ignore the self-defeating thoughts of lower self, and to have trust in my higher self and in God's divine plan for me. I reluctantly accepted because my lower self's voice was on a loudspeaker. It kept influencing me to think I was overwhelmed with just beginning to recover from the trauma of the stroke.

I continued to struggle with the decision to remain in the course right up until discharge day. That day arrived in November. I had set the goal to start working on my university assignments in January 2005. When I opened my first textbook, I discovered that I had no attention span and could not concentrate on a single written word. To make it worse, I couldn't comprehend what I read nor retain anything I read. I panicked that the part of my brain responsible for reading comprehension was permanently damaged.

As a teacher, I have worked with many students who struggled with these skills and I remembered how frustrating it was for them. I assumed I was now in the same situation, helpless and frustrated. I did not have the emotional energy nor the strength to face the possibility of this additional permanent brain damage.

Once again, there was the strong temptation to withdraw from the course. Lower self said loud and clear, "This is too much work. You just had a stroke. This is stressful." I still doubted Stella's original muscle test so this time, I muscle-tested myself but had the same results: to remain in the course. Stella kindly re-muscle-tested me and had the same results. She encouraged me to trust my higher self, to have faith that I would receive what was necessary to complete the course, and to believe it would work out well.

My fears and worries were consuming me so I decided to pray for increased self-trust and that I would get through this. I also decided to offer to God any anxieties as they appeared. Slowly, when my reading comprehension started to improve, worries about this began to dissolve and so did any anxieties about not being able to complete the assignments.

I challenged my brain synapses to activate themselves with the goals to improve reading comprehension enough to understand the textbooks and later to write my papers. Almost every afternoon in January, I read and re-read the assigned university texts. I had to tackle reading in short chunks of time because reading was exhausting and added to my organic fatigue. It began with reading a sentence at least three times until I understood it. Then I read each paragraph at least three times. Following that, I sometimes re-read entire chapters twice. After two months of persistent daily reading, I managed to understand and remember what I had read to learn the content required to write four term papers in the following two months. Feeling productive and relieved, I regained my reading skills which made me feel blessed because a major milestone had been accomplished.

The next set of obstacles were easier to overcome yet still challenging. Typing 60 wpm was no longer a dance my left fingers could easily perform in partnership with the right hand. Fortunately, to overcome this, I had a new laptop with a writing tablet and dictation software. My university professor allowed generous extensions for all my assignments, which relieved the pressure from submitting all four assignments on their original due dates. Throughout those months, I remained calm by focusing only on the task of the day and living in the now. Sometimes, one day at a time was too much. Therefore, my focus had to be on one page at a time. I also struggled to stop giving in to my lower self to set unreasonable deadlines for each reading and writing task. To give in to giving up would have set me up for failure when clearly I was beginning to succeed with giving it my all.

Every time I experienced doubt and lack of self-trust in completing the course, I prayed to God. On the days I did not feel like reading or writing, I would ask for the desire to read, the ability to understand what I had read, and the persistence to write. I was always amazed, thrilled, and relieved with all my regained reading skills. I admired how much work I was able to accomplish in writing my papers on the days when I did not feel like writing. I was also relieved not to feel the burden of guilt when I was not doing coursework. Instead, I listened and believed my higher self that all would go well and it did. I experienced an unexpected comfort in knowing that all the assignments would be done in due time. My answered prayers blessed me with self-trust, calmness, and confidence. In the end, I succeeded with a B+ as a final grade, even though it was not my usual A. The satisfaction of completing the course against many odds was much sweeter than having an A. I felt blessed and excited about accomplishing normal tasks of the past.

I now understand why the muscle test was indicating it was in my best interest to complete the course. My brain had to relearn reading comprehension skills. It now is understandable why I had no more passion or interest for reading while I was in the hospital. Had I withdrawn from the university course, I probably would not have discovered the stroke-acquired reading deficits for quite some time. Who knows what length of time it would have taken to recreate or strengthen new brain pathways once I discovered the deficits. Possibly, it would have been more than the one month it actually took to overcome them.

I am grateful to have had the encouragement of Louis and Stella and my higher self. This experience taught me that listening to my inner voice does not have to initially make sense or be logical. In fact, in retrospect, the logic or reason for completing the course only became clear to me later on. Retraining my brain to concentrate and retain what I read was the real purpose for completing the course. It was not for the sake of finishing one more course as I thought it was.

The course was the vehicle for me to discover and correct my reading deficits. Through this whole process, I learned that sometimes to have faith is to have blind trust before knowing the whys or the hows.

Let's consider how geniuses use their intuitions to guide them in their discoveries and their quests for knowledge. Think of Albert Einstein before he made his discoveries. He had no proof or evidence about his hypotheses. He operated on what he intuitively knew, and he listened to his inner voice of deep knowledge like so many other discoverers and scientists did. They first believed without knowing the answers, then, with hard work and self-trust, they discovered the evidence or proof to validate their theories giving credibility to their inner knowing and intelligence. Although I'm no genius, I discovered through blind faith why I had to finish my university course, which at first seemed to me to be an insurmountable challenge.

Protecting Children's Openness to Higher Self & the "Unexplained"

As a child, I was blessed to be in tune with my higher self and to have awareness that granted me insights beyond my years. For example, I was just a toddler when I knew it best to leave my parents apartment while they had an argument related to my father's drinking. I would sit on our front porch steps and looked up at the sky. Immediately, I saw more than white, fluffy clouds set below a backdrop of a soft, clear blue sky. Beneath it were the deep forest green leaves of majestic trees gently flowing with the soothing wind. The birds' songs soothed my upset heart and the sun's rays embraced my body. In that moment, I saw a whole universe bigger than I and even though I was small, I was part of it all and knew I was vital to everything. What my parents were experiencing wasn't mine and it didn't matter because my soul was elated to know insight had blessed me with hope for wonderful things to happen. That memory continues to inspire me and remind me that I am an important being in this world no matter what surrounds me, and I must never give up.

I've since had many opportunities to discover my intuitive self while discovering a universe of fascinating happenings. I also believe as an adult if we remain open to experiences, we can see them as children do, life-enriching situations and even as mini-life miracles. All too often, children alone experience these marvelous things.

Can you recall as a child feeling fascination, gratitude, and excitement about an event that seemed amazing, mystical, and even miraculous? Seeing something as simple as God's face in the clouds on a day when you feel alone can be reassuring. The innocent child would see this as God's being there with him, and so would a receptive adult. I recall a road trip to visit persons in crisis close to another family and mine. There were signs with the message "Jesus is here with you" on trucks and there were far-away crosses, easy to overlook, along the road to our destination, but I saw them. When I pointed this out, one of the other adults later shared my view that Jesus was letting us know he was by our side. Indeed, he was, and we were able to get through an unimaginable and deeply disturbing event. We all somehow found our own ways to come to terms with the reality—even with a little humor.

As we grow older, we somehow lose sight of this childlike ability to recognize and appreciate life's wondrous mini-miracles. At some point, as we grow older, our expectations of miraculous events blind us from recognizing mini-miracles and we lose sight of how they can make a significant impact on our lives. They are evidence of how our lives have many subtle, divine interventions. If we are open to accept and appreciate them, they have the potential to give us renewed hope and faith.

When I was growing up, several adults unintentionally negated what I told them I had seen or experienced by making absolute statements that my mini-miracles were not possibilities. This inadvertently influenced me to doubt my inner voice and to shy away from developing my psychic abilities further. This meant I sometimes tuned out my ears' attunement to my soul's gentle, loving wisdom because I no longer had trust in what I experienced.

Every time an adult is unaware of divine circumstances in a child's life and responds with statements implying that the child is imagining things, being silly, or making things up, the child gradually mutes his inner voice closing his soul's lens. When an adult tells a child it is not possible to see or hear a dead grandparent, the adult influences the child to not only doubt his experiences but to miss out on the rich experience of a divine, healing encounter.

Many adults in our world function in ways that rely mostly on concrete practicality, logic, and reason. This prevents them from realizing that children can be messengers of God or the divine universe. When these golden opportunities are overlooked, divine blessings are lost. For example, the day my family learned that my estranged father had died, Christian was not yet four years old. That evening, my sister Denise and I shared our grief with our maternal grandparents and Christian. Dan was flying in from Atlanta.

After supper, as I was driving home with Christian in the back seat, I began to cry when stopped at a red light.

Christian calmly asked me, "Maman, are you crying because of your dad?" I answered yes and he continued to say in a sincere, calm reassuring voice, "But he says it is okay. He is okay!"

We're often so blind. Our demand for the credentialed so colors our perception of believability, that we would not recognize God if he appeared within us.—Anonymous

My initial response was to verbally correct him and tell him that did not make sense because for an instant, I was operating from my left brain. I almost scolded him for being silly, it was not funny, that my father could not be talking to him. He was dead. Fortunately, I remembered when I saw my mémère Emond after she died, and then a friend who died at eighteen, both telling me what I needed to hear. Mémère had let me know she was by my side and my friend had let me know she was safe in heaven. Then I thought of my prayers hours earlier asking God that he take my father by his side in heaven and keep his soul safe.

I was worried about my chronic, alcoholic father's soul not going to heaven because he had been unable to be a responsible, reliable, and healthy husband and father. It disturbed me greatly that this man, who was not born out of love, had never experienced unconditional love other than from his mother and then had died without knowing the joy of a life filled with love. This was unfair and I wouldn't believe he'd be condemned because he'd abused his life and others' lives.

Thinking about my prayers to God asking for mercy for my father's soul, I realized that Christian's comment was my answer. Instead of having an automatic response by scolding him for saying silly things, I thanked Christian for sharing this important message with me. I asked him to repeat what he'd said.

"He says he is okay. He is all right."

In that instant, I realized Christian's innocent soul was the receptive vehicle for my father to communicate to me what I desperately needed to know. He was, indeed, at peace with God. I immediately felt an overwhelming relief with the reassurance that his soul was no longer suffering as it had on earth. I now knew that my father's soul was safe with God.

Throughout the early weeks following my father's death, I was comforted several times with feeling his presence close by. For example, during the funeral arrangement meeting with the funeral director, something strong in me made me pronounce before I could think about it, "I'll sing Amazing Grace." I was surprised those words had come out of my mouth and that no one tried to talk me out of it. I later found out that my father had loved this song. I learned the lyrics within a few days and sang it a cappella at his funeral. I believe my unexpected urge to sing at his funeral was inspired by him from beyond because under no other circumstances would I have offered to sing at a funeral let alone a cappella. My father had a natural musical talent to play guitar as well as sing his favorite country songs. Recognizing his passion, I realized I did what he would have wanted, and thus honored his passion for singing music.

These spiritual experiences with my father and Christian are a beautiful reminder for me to listen carefully to those strong pulses of inspiration and to children, because I never know when they might be the vehicles of divine insights, learning, and blessings. I want to remain open to my inner voice and to those of the children in my life. Most importantly, I must listen to and validate their experiences so they will continue to receive messages as intended. As adults, we may not realize that we are inadvertently teaching our children not to be aware of and to trust their inner voice. Learning to listen to our soul is our connection to universal truths and to divine answers.

In the attitude of silence the soul finds the path in a clearer light,
and what is elusive and deceptive resolves itself into crystal
clearness. Our life is a long and arduous quest after Truth.
—Mahatma Gandhi

Meditation and Prayer to Higher Self

Through daily meditation and prayer, I learned to familiarize myself with my higher self's voice and gained confidence to discern its voice from that of the lower self. I reacquainted myself with my soul through a specific meditation focusing on the heart and crown chakras called meditation on twin hearts that I had learned in Pranic Healing. [Kok Sui, Meditation on Twin Hearts with Self-Pranic Healing, 2000] This heightens my intuitive awareness so that I can clearly hear and know the voice of higher self, making God's presence ever more felt. I also began to gain new insights about my behaviors, thought patterns, and true purpose in life. Not only did my relationship with God deepen, but so did many of my familial, personal, and other relationships improve as well. Since beginning this practice, I learned how letting go of this routine hurts me. I fall into old patterns of thought and behavior that do not honor my true self. I lose centeredness, and am not present in all my bodies. When this happens, it's my cue to get back on track to daily meditation and prayer.

This makes me think that there is not one prescribed way to get in tune with our higher self, to learn how to have faith in God and to develop self-trust. It is a journey that is personal and based on individual needs and experiences. There are many dogmas, religions, methodologies, and practices to choose from that are available to help us. Everyone needs to find her appropriate and suitable way of practicing her faith in her God or higher being. What worked for me may not necessarily work for the next person. For those interested, I suggest you tune in to your higher self, practice meditation, mindfulness, prayer, and spend quiet time with self. The activities might be helpful toward hearing and recognizing your soul's voice.

The Gifts of GEMS

Gifts surround us in plain packages that can so easily be taken for granted. They can be kind loving gestures, a helping hand, or a poster's words perfectly stated to give hope. Since my stroke, I look for those gifts that inspire hope to brighten, to lighten my days, to strengthen my faith, and to maintain my joie de vivre. It is a choice to either be blind and remain bitter or to open my eyes and be grateful. These gifts are easier to see when I choose a healthy and positive perspective. I will share in alphabetical order the most significant gifts I experienced throughout my stroke journey and since learned how important they are for everyday living. I am certain there are many other gifts I have neglected to include in this chapter. However, these are the most critical ones that helped me get through stroke recovery.

Gift of Anger

Ironic as it seems, anger was a gift. Anger forced me to face what I needed to see and motivated me to find the courage and strength to take action where necessary. From my anger came awareness and this awareness empowered me to make choices, which in turn, gave me the power to transform myself, to move forward without blame and complaint and to forgive when necessary.

Ask and it shall be given you; seek and ye shall find; knock, and it shall be opened unto you.—Bible: Matthew (7:7)

Gift of Faith

Much of this book explains how my faith is essential to my harmonious living. Therefore, I don't need to elaborate anymore on the topic. However, I'd like to say I keep receiving the precious gift of continued faith every time I ask God to help me get through all ordeals. He is ever present in my life through the GEMS, kind gestures and words, and timely calls from loved ones reaching out to me, especially when I am in difficult places.

Gift of Forgiveness

In the past, conflict with a friend or family member usually meant I lost affection for them and sometimes had lingering anger toward them. My near-death experience opened the opportunity for me to practice genuine forgiveness and a chance to change positively my interactions with others.

Gift of Inner Strength

I always had an inner strength that carried me through many critical life-changing events. However, the stroke was like no other. An inner strength I never thought I had, emerged from the deepest recesses of darkness. I found strength to face my losses, and to do the daily exhausting, intensive physical therapy for a solid four years. There is the internal and physical strength to stand up independently from my wheelchair, walk several feet without a cane, hold an object in my left hand again, or walk without an AFO.

Gift of Joy from Laughter

Emotional incontinence brought my family many joyous moments. I tackled life's inconveniences and frustrations with humor and laughter as I had never done before. It became easy to accept the emotional incontinence as a gift because it taught my family, and me, to laugh more, to suck it up and move on. What used to be problems became minor annoyances and inconveniences not worth wasting precious energy on. We couldn't control them so why not laugh.

The emotional incontinence I inherited blessed me with a couple of years of uncontrollable laughter at a time when stroke recovery was the most exhausting, demanding, and daunting. I am thankful for the gift of irrepressible laughter at a time when there was very little or no apparent reasons for joy. I must say, this is the most pleasant side effect of brain damage. While in the rehab hospital, I had many impulsive outbursts of laughter that were infectious to those around me. Whenever I felt self-pity beginning to erupt, I would try to find something funny that would help me drown it in laughter. In those situations, self-pity had no choice but to take a back seat to laughter and joy.

It's not whether you get knocked down. It's whether you get up again.—Vince Lombardi

Gift of Life

I believe the first gift I received after the stroke was the drug tPA that spared me from having more harmful strokes so therefore, extended my physical life. My sacred contract's blueprint is to serve God and give testimony of my many journeys. I also believe that my blueprint included having a stroke as a catalyst to help me understand and fulfill my soul's mission.

Gift of Love

The blessing in having a receptive heart opened my eyes to see the love I received and to accept it willingly and freely. It gave me increased quality of life, support and strength during the stroke grieving process. I am grateful that God gave me Louis who was lovingly attentive, dedicated and nurturing in ways I had not experienced before my stroke. I felt very fortunate that Louis was a strong man who did not run away from his suddenly disabled wife who no longer was the same woman physically that he had married.

Family, friends, colleagues, church members, and the community, truly are blessings of support and encouragement during times of crisis. I experienced unconditional love from all these people. There was no other way I wanted to interpret all this love than as God's way of showing me his presence in my life. All this bountiful love increased my faith in God, confirmed that he had not abandoned me, nor punished me. Everyone's love gave me the strength and courage to face the daunting road ahead.

Gift of Pranic Healing

The energy healing practices and skills I learned from Pranic Healing benefited my family and me in countless profound ways. First, it gave me immediate skills to manage my tendonitis pain and migraine headaches. I learned valuable esoteric teachings and the best gift is the twin hearts meditation including all the other guided meditations that keep me in a healthy state of mind. I thank GrandMaster Choa

Kok Sui for translating ancient, esoteric teachings for the benefit of all humanity.

Gift of Reclaiming Mother–Child Relationship

My childhood circumstances molded me to be self-reliant and independent. These are good qualities but I took them to the limit. At a very young age, I observed that my mother was heavily burdened with worries and responsibilities related to my father's alcoholism. When she became a single parent, she was very much occupied with raising us three children on a fixed income. I felt her plate was full, so at some point in my childhood, I concluded I needed to be there to assist her in any way I could. It is since then that I never allowed myself to depend on my mother.

My stroke taught me how to be my mother's child. It provided her the opportunity to be a mother and to nurture me for the first time in many decades. I could accept this guilt free. It was a therapeutic, cathartic healing for both of us to be finally mother and daughter in our respective roles.

Gift of Support

I felt truly blessed and fortunate to have so many people in my life who attended to my needs: my primary caregivers, Louis, my mother, and my children; other family members; and many very close friends, all were instrumental supporters toward my recovery.

My vulnerabilities were in no way anyone's responsibility but my own. I recognize how difficult it must have been for my family and friends to witness my losses, pain, and suffering. Thankfully, people I love were committed to seeing and acting on my need for support. This realization helped me feel even more gratitude for their inner strength in staying with me to share my losses, sorrows, and joys. They were in no way obliged to be with me, but I know it was their choice to be there for me. That gave me tremendous courage and stamina.

Gift of Time

Time is precious. Before the stroke, I never had enough time for many things outside of my career, including quality family time and rest. There was a time when I would have said I'd do anything for free time to do my creative projects. Well, I never imagined I'd have this time but with no interest, desire or able-body to do them. At first, all I could do aside from physical therapy was lie in exhaustion on the couch. After a couple of months of this, I began to feel guilty. Once I was on antidepressants, the guilt disappeared because I could think clearly. My new job now was to rest and heal my body. I gave myself permission to sleep most of the day in the beginning because simple, daily activities physically exhausted me. Between the countless naps, I enjoyed watching Oprah and Dr. Phil on TV; a habit I began when I was in the hospital. It was helpful to see other people's lives; their crises helped me to see I wasn't alone with a cross to bear.

After I regained my reading comprehension ability, I enjoyed reading all the books I wanted to without feeling guilty. I justified the time spent reading by rationalizing that I was physically limited so I might as well learn more about life by reading inspirational and healing books. I remember one day thinking as I lay on the couch reading all afternoon how lucky I was because I had always dreamed of having free time to read. And here I was doing it!

I used this time to not only read but also to reflect, meditate and write this book. As my body got stronger and I could do more, I had less time but more mental energy to read. I also no longer felt justified in taking the time to read for several hours on the couch as I had in the early months of my recovery. I used that time to relearn how to do daily activities. My stroke also afforded me the gift of time away from work to dedicate my attention to writing this book, to focus on my soul, and to engage more actively in living my purpose while recovering from my stroke.

Closing Thoughts

Many before me have and many more will have to walk the arduous journey of stroke recovery or other life crises. The effects of stroke on the survivors and their loved ones are not always evident to observers. This is of no fault to the observer but simply put, you can never know what people have experienced or have lost unless you walk for a while in their shoes or examine the footprints they have left behind for all to witness. A person's pain and sorrow is not so evident until they have chosen a path that clearly reveals his crisis. There is also the situation of sudden paralysis or of a lost limb. Truly, you can not know what you got until it's literally gone. My paralyzing stroke was not a scolding lesson, but a compassionate, loving lesson about faith, self-trust, love, and finding divine direction on the path toward achieving purpose and fulfilling my sacred contract. I end with my quote I use in all my speaking presentations. God bless.

> *What I once was*
> *Is gone forever,*
> *What I am today*
> *Is temporary,*
> *And what I will be tomorrow*
> *Is what I make of it.*—Carole Laurin

Bibliography

Bernie S. Siegel, M. (2004). *Meditations for Difficult Times: How to Survive and Thrive.*

Bernie S. Siegel, M. (1989). *Peace, Love & Healing: Bodymind Communication & the Path to Self-Healing an Exploration.* New York: Harper & Row.

Braden, G. (2008). *The Divine Matrix: Bridging Time, Space, Miracles, and Belief.* USA.

Braden, G. (2008). *The Spontaneous Healing of Belief: Shattering the Paradigm of False Limits.* USA.

Chopra, F. W. (2010). *The Shadow Effect: Illuminating the Hidden Power of Your True Self.* USA.

Cloosterman, A. (2011). *The Difference between Thinking and Thought.* Retrieved on October 2, 2013, from Mindstructures: http://www.mindstructures.com/2011/01/the-difference-between-thinking-and-thought/ David D. Burns, M. (1999). *The Feeling Good Handbook.* New York: The Penguin Group.

Dickens, C. (1843). *A Christmas Carol.* London, England: Chapman and Hall.

Dr. D. Ramesh, M. A. (2006). *Digital Brain Mapping Study.* Chennai.

Dyer, D. W. (2001). *There is a Spiritual Solution to Every Problem.* USA.

Dyer, W. (2004). *The Power of Intention.* USA.

Emoto, M. (2004). *The Hidden Messages in Water.* Hillsboro, Oregon: Beyond Words Publishing.

Ford, D. (2002). *The Dark Side of the Light Chasers: Reclaiming Your Power, Creativity, Brilliance, and Dreams.* New York: Riverhead Books.

Ford, D. (1998). *The Dark Side of the Light Chasers: Reclaiming Your Power, Creativity, Brilliance, and Dreams.* New York: Riverhead Books.

Ford, D. (2008). *Why Good People Do Bad Things: How to Stop Being Your Own Worst Enemy.* New York: Harper One.

Goorrjian, M. (Director). (2009). *The Shift* [Motion Picture].

Hawkins, D. R. (2002). *Power vs Force—The Hidden Determinants of Human Behavior.* Carlsbad, USA: Hay House, Inc.

Hay, L. (2004). *Anger Releasing.* USA.

Hay, L. (2005). *Dissolving Barriers: Discover Your Subconscious Blocks to Love, Health, and a Powerful Self-Image.* USA.

Hay, L. (2004). *Stress-Free: Peaceful Affirmations to Relieve Anxiety and Help You Relax.* USA.

Hay, L. (1999). *You Can Heal Your Life.* USA: Hay House.

Kell, T. (2004). *Chain of Miracles: Journey through Faith.* Canada: Tate Publishing.

Klassen, J. A. *Transformative Writing.*

Klassen, J. (2003). *Tools of Transformation: Write Your Way to New Worlds of Possibilities in Just 5 Minutes.* Winnipeg: Panama Press Canada—A Heartspace Publication.

Kok Sui, M. C. (2000). *Meditation on Twin Hearts with Self-Pranic Healing.* Paramus, New Jersey, USA: Aquarian Visions, Inc.

Kok Sui, M. C. (1998). *Miracles through Pranic Healing.* Philippines: Institute For Inner Studies.

Kubler-Ross, E. (1969). *On Death and Dying.* New York: Macmillan PublishingCompany, Inc.

Lama, D. (Mar 6 1995). *The Power of Compassion.* Toronto: HarperCollins Canada/Thorsons.

Lama, T. D. (1995). *The Power of Compassion.* New Dehli: HarperCollins.

Meyer, C. (2012). *Emotions versus Feelings.* Retrieved on October 3, 2013, from The Emotional Detective: http://emotionaldetective.typepad.com/emotional-detective/2012/04/emotions-vs-feelings.html

Myss, C. (2001). *Advanced Energy Anatomy: The Science of Co-Creation and Your Power of Choice.* USA.

Myss, C. (1996). *Anatomy of the Spirit.* New York: Three Rivers Press.

Myss, C. (2009). *Defy Gravity: Healing Beyond the Bounds of Reason.* USA, USA: Hay House.

Myss, C. (2007). *Entering the Castle: An Inner Path to God and Your Soul.* New York: Free Press.

Myss, C. (2002). *Sacred Contract.* New York, USA: Three Rivers Press.

Myss, C. (2004). *The Call to Live a Symbolic Life.* USA.

Myss, C. (2006, January 26). *The Language of Archetypes: Discover the Forces that Shape Your Destiny.* Louisville, CO, USA: Sounds True.

Peale, N. V. (1969). *The Power of Positive Thinking.* New York: Fawcett World Library.

Rama, S. (n.d.). *Emotions, Mind, and Ego.* Retrieved August 19, 2012, from *Traditional Yoga and Meditation of the Himalayan Masters*: http://www.swamij.com/swami-rama-emotions-mind.htm

Rama, S. (n.d.). *The Spiritual Layers of Man.* Retrieved August 19, 2012, from *House of the Sun*: http://www.soul-guidance.com/houseofthesun/spirituallayers.htm

Reynolds, M. (2007). *Feelings vs Emotions*. Retrieved October 3, 2013, from Outsmart Your Brain: http://outsmartyourbrain. com/2007/12/27/feelings-vs-emotions/#sthash.4z0b7Gie.dpuf

Scott Peck, M. (1978). *The Road Less Traveled: A New Psychology of Love, Traditional Values and Spiritual Growth*. New York: Simon & Schuster.

Tolle, E. (2005). *A New Earth: Awakening to Your Life's Purpose*. USA: Plume.

Vanzant, I. (2012, April 13). *Oprah and the Oprah's Lifeclass: the Tour Teachers Live from Toronto: The Power of Forgiveness*. (Oprah, Interviewer)

Virtue, D. (2000). *Divine Prescriptions: Using Your Sixth Sense— Spiritual Solutions for You and Your Loved Ones*. New York: St. Martin's Griffin.

Warren, R. (2002). *The Purpose Driven Life: What on Earth Am I Here For?* Grand Rapids, Mich, USA: Zondervan.

Williams, T. S.-Z. (2007). *The Mindful Way through Depression*. New York: The Guilford Press.

Wolfensberger, W. (1998). *A Brief Introduction to Social Role Valorization: A High-Order Concept for Addressing the Plight of Societally Devalued People, and for Structuring Human Services* (3rd ed.). Syracuse, New York, USA: Training Institute for Human Service Planning, Leadership & Change Agentry (Syracuse University).

Young, W. P. (2007). *The Shack: Where Tragedy Confronts Eternity*. Newbury Park: Windblown Media.

Carole Laurin grew up in St. Boniface, the French quarter of Winnipeg, Manitoba. She now lives in Ottawa, Ontario, with her husband, Louis Barré, and children, Chloé and Christian. A former French immersion teacher, she now pursues her creative impulses in writing and painting, and advocates for improved patient care and is a spokesperson for stroke survivors.